By Agnes Repplier

AMERICANS AND OTHERS.

A HAPPY HALF-CENTURY AND OTHER ESSAYS.

IN OUR CONVENT DAYS.

COMPROMISES.

THE FIRESIDE SPHINX. With 4 full-page and 17 text Illustrations by Miss E. BONSALL.

BOOKS AND MEN.

POINTS OF VIEW

ESSAYS IN IDLENESS.

IN THE DOZY HOURS, AND OTHER PAPERS.

ESSAYS IN MINIATURE.

A BOOK OF FAMOUS VERSE. Selected by Agnes Repplier. In Riverside Library for Young People.

THE SAME. *Holiday Edition.*

VARIA.

HOUGHTON MIFFLIN COMPANY
BOSTON AND NEW YORK

AMERICANS AND OTHERS

AMERICANS AND OTHERS

BY

AGNES REPPLIER, Litt.D.

BOSTON AND NEW YORK
HOUGHTON MIFFLIN COMPANY
The Riverside Press Cambridge
1912

Published October 1912

Note

FIVE of the essays in this volume appear in print for the first time. Others have been published in the *Atlantic Monthly*, the *Century Magazine*, *Harper's Bazar*, and the *Catholic World*.

Contents

AMERICANS AND OTHERS

A Question of Politeness

"La politesse de l'esprit consiste à penser des choses honnêtes et délicates."

A GREAT deal has been said and written during the past few years on the subject of American manners, and the consensus of opinion is, on the whole, unfavourable. We have been told, more in sorrow than in anger, that we are not a polite people; and our critics have cast about them for causes which may be held responsible for such a universal and lamentable result. Mr. Thomas Nelson Page, for example, is by way of thinking that the fault lies in the sudden expansion of wealth, in the intrusion into the social world of people who fail to understand its requirements, and in the universal "spoiling" of American children. He contrasts the South of his childhood, that wonderful "South before the war," which looms vaguely, but very grandly, through a half-century's haze, with the New York of to-day, which, alas! has nothing to soften its outlines. A more censorious critic in the "Atlantic Monthly" has also stated explicitly that for true consideration and courtliness we must hark back to certain old gentlewomen of ante-bellum days. "None of us born since the Civil War approach them in respect to some fine, nameless quality that gives them charm and atmosphere." It would seem, then, that the war, with its great emotions and its sustained heroism, imbued us with national life at the expense of our national manners.

I wonder if this kind of criticism does not err by comparing the many with the few, the general with the exceptional. I wonder if the deficiencies of an imperfect civilization can be accounted for along such obvious lines. The self-absorption of youth which Mrs. Comer deprecates, the self-absorption of a crowd which offends Mr. Page, are human, not American. The nature of youth and the nature of crowds have not changed essentially since the Civil War, nor since the Punic Wars. Granted that the tired and hungry citizens of New York, jostling one another in their efforts to board a homeward train, present an unlovely spectacle; but do they, as Mr. Page affirms, reveal "such sheer and primal brutality as can be found nowhere else in the world where men and women are together?" Crowds will jostle, and have always jostled, since men first clustered in communities. Read Theocritus. The hurrying Syracusans — third century B.C. — "rushed like a herd of swine," and rent in twain Praxinoë's muslin veil. Look at Hogarth. The whole fun of an eighteenth-century English crowd consisted in snatching off some unfortunate's wig, or toppling him over into the gutter. The truth is we sin against civilization when we consent to flatten ourselves against our neighbours. The experience of the world has shown conclusively that a few inches more or less of breathing space make all the difference between a self-respecting citizen and a savage.

As for youth, — ah, who shall be brave enough, who has ever been brave enough, to defend the rising generation? Who has ever looked with content upon the young, save only Plato, and he lived in an age of symmetry and order which we can hardly hope to reproduce. The shortcomings of youth are so pitilessly, so glaringly apparent. Not a rag to cover them from the discerning eye. And what a veil has fallen between us and the years of *our* offending. There is no illusion so permanent as that which enables us to look backward with complacency; there is no mental process so deceptive as the comparing of recollections with realities. How loud and shrill the voice of the girl at our elbow. How soft the voice which from the far past breathes its gentle echo in our ears. How bouncing the vigorous young creatures who surround us, treading us under foot in the certainty of their self-assurance. How sweet and reasonable the pale shadows who smile — we think appealingly — from some dim corner of our memories. There is a passage in the diary of Louisa Gurney, a carefully reared little Quaker girl of good family and estate, which is dated 1796, and which runs thus: —

"I was in a very playing mood to-day, and thoroughly enjoyed being foolish, and tried to be as rude to everybody as I could. We went on the highroad for the purpose of being rude to the folks that passed. I do think being rude is most pleasant sometimes."

Let us hope that the grown-up Louisa Gurney, whenever she felt disposed to cavil at the imperfections of the rising generation of 1840 or 1850, re-read these illuminating words, and softened her judgment accordingly.

New York has been called the most insolent city in the world. To make or to refute such a statement implies so wide a knowledge of contrasted civilizations that to most of us the words have no significance. It is true that certain communities have earned for themselves in the course of centuries an unenviable reputation for discourtesy. The Italians say "as rude as a Florentine"; and even the casual tourist (presuming his standard of manners to have been set by Italy) is disposed to echo the reproach. The Roman, with the civilization of the world at his back, is naturally, one might say inevitably, polite. His is that serious and simple dignity which befits his high inheritance. But the Venetian and the Sienese have also a grave courtesy of bearing, compared with which the manners of the Florentine seem needlessly abrupt. We can no more account for this than we can account for the churlishness of the Vaudois, who is always at some pains to be rude, and the gentleness of his neighbour, the Valaisan, to whom breeding is a birthright, born, it would seem, of generosity of heart, and a scorn of ignoble things.

But such generalizations, at all times perilous, become impossible in the changing currents of American life, which has as yet no quality of permanence. The delicate old tests fail to adjust themselves to our needs. Mr. Page is right theoretically when he says that the treatment of a servant or of a subordinate is an infallible criterion of manners, and when he rebukes the "arrogance" of wealthy women to "their hapless sisters of toil." But the truth is that our hapless sisters of toil have things pretty much their own way in a country which is still broadly prosperous and democratic, and our treatment of them is tempered by a selfish consideration for our own comfort and convenience. If they are toiling as domestic servants, — a field in which the demand exceeds the supply, — they hold the key to the situation; it is sheer foolhardiness to be arrogant to a cook. Dressmakers and milliners are not humbly seeking for patronage; theirs is the assured position of people who can give the world what the world asks; and as for saleswomen, a class upon whom much sentimental sympathy is lavished year by year, their heart-whole superciliousness to the poor shopper, especially if she chance to be a housewife striving nervously to make a few dollars cover her family needs, is wantonly and detestably unkind. It is not with us as it was in the England of Lamb's day, and the quality of breeding is shown in a well-practised restraint rather than in a sweet and somewhat lofty consideration.

Eliminating all the more obvious features of criticism, as throwing no light upon the subject, we come to the consideration of three points,— the domestic, the official, and the social manners of a nation which has been roundly accused of degenerating from the high standard of former years, of those gracious and beautiful years which few of us have the good fortune to remember. On the first count, I believe that a candid and careful observation will result in a verdict of acquittal. Foreigners, Englishmen and Englishwomen especially, who visit our shores, are impressed with the politeness of Americans in their own households. That fine old Saxon point of view, "What is the good of a family, if one cannot be disagreeable in the bosom of it?" has been modified by the simple circumstance that the family bosom is no longer a fixed and permanent asylum. The disintegration of the home may be a lamentable feature of modern life; but since it has dawned upon our minds that adult members of a family need not necessarily live together if they prefer to live apart, the strain of domesticity has been reduced to the limits of endurance. We have gained in serenity what we have lost in self-discipline by this easy achievement of an independence which, fifty years ago, would have been deemed pure licence. I can remember that, when I was a little girl, two of our neighbours, a widowed mother and a widowed daughter, scandalized all their friends by living in two large comfortable houses, a stone's throw apart, instead of under one roof as became their relationship; and the fact that they loved each other dearly and peacefully in no way lessened their transgression. Had they shared their home, and bickered day and night, that would have been considered unfortunate but "natural."

If the discipline of family life makes for law and order, for the subordination of parts to the whole, and for the prompt recognition of authority; if, in other words, it makes, as in the days of Rome, for citizenship, the rescue of the individual makes for social intercourse, for that temperate and reasoned attitude which begets courtesy. The modern mother may lack influence and authority; but she speaks more urbanely to her children than her mother spoke to her. The modern child is seldom respectful, but he is often polite, with a politeness which owes nothing to intimidation. The harsh and wearisome habit of contradiction, which used to be esteemed a family privilege, has been softened to a judicious dissent. In my youth I knew several old gentlemen who might, on their death-beds, have laid their hands upon their hearts, and have sworn that never in their whole lives had they permitted any statement, however insignificant, to pass uncontradicted in their presence. They were authoritative old gentlemen, kind husbands after their fashion, and careful fathers; but conversation at their dinner-tables was not for human delight.

The manners of American officials have been discussed with more or less acrimony, and always from the standpoint of personal experience. The Custom-House is the centre of attack, and critics for the most part agree that the men whose business it is to "hold up" returning citizens perform their ungracious task ungraciously. Theirs is rather the attitude of the detective dealing with suspected criminals than the attitude of the public servant impersonally obeying orders. It is true that even on the New York docks one may encounter civility and kindness. There are people who assure us that they have never encountered anything else; but then there are people who would have us believe that always and under all circumstances they meet with the most distinguished consideration. They intimate that there is *that* in their own demeanour which makes rudeness to them an impossibility.

More candid souls find it hard to account for the crudity of our intercourse, not with officials only, but with the vast world which lies outside our narrow circle of associates. We have no human relations where we have no social relations; we are awkward and constrained in our recognition of the unfamiliar; and this awkwardness encumbers us in the ordinary routine of life. A policeman who has been long on one beat, and who has learned to know either the householders or the business men of his locality, is wont to be the most friendly of mortals. There is something almost pathetic in the value he places upon human relationship, even of a very casual order. A conductor on a local train who has grown familiar with scores of passengers is no longer a ticket-punching, station-shouting automaton. He bears himself in friendly fashion towards all travellers, because he has established with some of them a rational foothold of communication. But the official who sells tickets to a hurrying crowd, or who snaps out a few tart words at a bureau of information, or who guards a gate through which men and women are pushing with senseless haste, is clad in an armour of incivility. He is wantonly rude to foreigners, whose helplessness should make some appeal to his humanity. I have seen a gate-keeper at Jersey City take by the shoulders a poor German, whose ticket called for another train, and shove him roughly out of the way, without a word of explanation. The man, too bewildered for resentment, rejoined his wife to whom he had said good-bye, and the two anxious, puzzled creatures stood whispering together as the throng swept callously past them. It was a painful spectacle, a lapse from the well-ordered decencies of civilization.

For to be civilized is to be incapable of giving unnecessary offence, it is to have some quality of consideration for all who cross our path. An Englishwoman once said to Mr. Whistler that the politeness of the French was "all on the surface," to which the artist made reply: "And a very good place for it to be." It is this sweet surface politeness, costing so little, counting for so much, which smooths the roughness out of life. "The classic quality of the French nation," says Mr. Henry James, "is sociability; a sociability which operates in France, as it never does in England, from below upward. Your waiter utters a greeting because, after all, something human within him prompts him. His instinct bids him say something, and his taste recommends that it should be agreeable."

This combination of instinct and taste — which happily is not confined to the French, nor to waiters — produces some admirable results, results out of all proportion to the slightness of the means employed. It often takes but a word, a gesture, to indicate the delicate process of adjustment. A few summers ago I was drinking tea with friends in the gardens of the Hotel Faloria, at Cortina. At a table near us sat two Englishmen, three Englishwomen, and an Austrian, the wife of a Viennese councillor. They talked with animation and in engaging accents. After a little while they arose and strolled back to the hotel. The Englishmen, as they passed our table, stared hard at two young girls who were of our party, stared as deliberately and with as much freedom as if the children had been on a London music-hall stage. The Englishwomen passed us as though we had been invisible. They had so completely the air of seeing nothing in our chairs that I felt myself a phantom, a ghost like Banquo's, with no guilty eye to discern my presence at the table. Lastly came the Austrian, who had paused to speak to a servant, and, as *she* passed, she gave us a fleeting smile and a slight bow, the mere shadow of a curtsey, acknowledging our presence as human beings, to whom some measure of recognition was due.

It was such a little thing, so lightly done, so eloquent of perfect self-possession, and the impression it made upon six admiring Americans was a permanent one. We fell to asking ourselves — being honestly conscious of constraint — how each one of us would have behaved in the Austrian lady's place, whether or not that act of simple and sincere politeness would have been just as easy for us. Then I called to mind one summer morning in New England, when I sat on a friend's piazza, waiting idly for the arrival of the Sunday papers. A decent-looking man, with a pretty and over-dressed girl by his side, drove up the avenue, tossed the packet of papers at our feet, and drove away again. He had not said even a bare "Good morning." My kind and courteous host had offered no word of greeting. The girl had turned her head to stare at me, but had not spoken. Struck by the ungraciousness of the whole episode, I asked, "Is he a stranger in these parts?"

"No," said my friend. "He has brought the Sunday papers all summer. That is his daughter with him."

All summer, and no human relations, not enough to prompt a friendly word, had been established between the man who served and the man who was served. None of the obvious criticisms passed upon American manners can explain the crudity of such a situation. It was certainly not a case of arrogance towards a hapless brother of toil. My friend probably toiled much harder than the paperman, and was the least arrogant of mortals. Indeed, all arrogance of bearing lay conspicuously on the paperman's part. Why, after all, should not his instinct, like the instinct of the French waiter, have bidden him say something; why should not his taste have recommended that the something be agreeable? And then, again, why should not my friend, in whom social constraint was unpardonable, have placed his finer instincts at the service of a fellow creature? We must probe to the depths of our civilization before we can understand and deplore the limitations which make it difficult for us to approach one another with mental ease and security. We have yet to learn that the amenities of life stand for its responsibilities, and translate them into action. They express externally the fundamental relations which ought to exist between men. "All the distinctions, so delicate and sometimes so complicated, which belong to good breeding," says M. Rondalet in "La Réforme Sociale," "answer to a profound unconscious analysis of the duties we owe to one another."

There are people who balk at small civilities on account of their manifest insincerity. They cannot be brought to believe that the expressions of unfelt pleasure or regret with which we accept or decline invitations, the little affectionate phrases which begin and end our letters, the agreeable formalities which have accumulated around the simplest actions of life, are beneficent influences upon character, promoting gentleness of spirit. The Quakers, as we know, made a mighty stand against verbal insincerities, with one striking exception, — the use of the word "Friend." They said and believed that this word represented their attitude towards humanity, their spirit of universal tolerance and brotherhood. But if to call oneself a "Friend" is to emphasize one's amicable relations towards one's neighbour, to call one's neighbour "Friend" is to imply that he returns this affectionate regard, which is often an unwarranted assumption. It is better and more logical to accept *all* the polite phraseology which facilitates intercourse, and contributes to the sweetness of life. If we discarded the formal falsehoods which are the currency of conversation, we should not be one step nearer the vital things of truth.

For to be sincere with ourselves is better and harder than to be painstakingly accurate with others. A man may be cruelly candid to his associates, and a cowardly hypocrite to himself. He may handle his friend harshly, and himself with velvet gloves. He may never tell the fragment of a lie, and never think the whole truth. He may wound the pride and hurt the feelings of all with whom he comes in contact, and never give his own soul the benefit of one good knockdown blow. The connection which has been established between rudeness and probity on the one hand, and politeness and insincerity on the other, is based upon an imperfect knowledge of human nature.

> "So rugged was he that we thought him just,
> So churlish was he that we deemed him true."

"It is better to hold back a truth," said

Saint Francis de Sales, "than to speak it ungraciously."

There are times doubtless when candour goes straight to its goal, and courtesy misses the mark. Mr. John Stuart Mill was once asked upon the hustings whether or not he had ever said that the English working-classes were mostly liars. He answered shortly, "I did!" — and the unexpected reply was greeted with loud applause. Mr. Mill was wont to quote this incident as proof of the value which Englishmen set upon plain speaking. They do prize it, and they prize the courage which defies their bullying. But then the remark was, after all, a generalization. We can bear hearing disagreeable truths spoken to a crowd or to a congregation — causticity has always been popular in preachers — because there are other heads than our own upon which to fit the cap.

The brutalities of candour, the pestilent wit which blights whatever it touches, are not distinctively American. It is because we are a humorous rather than a witty people that we laugh for the most part with, and not at, our fellow creatures. Indeed, judged by the unpleasant things we might say and do not say, we should be esteemed polite. English memoirs teem with anecdotes which appear to us unpardonable. Why should Lady Holland have been permitted to wound the susceptibilities of all with whom she came in contact? When Moore tells us that she said to him, "This book of yours" (the "Life of Sheridan") "will be dull, I fear;" and to Lord Porchester, "I am sorry to hear you are going to publish a poem. Can't you suppress it?" we do not find these remarks to be any more clever than considerate. They belong to the category of the monumentally uncouth.

Why should Mr. Abraham Hayward have felt it his duty (he put it that way) to tell Mr. Frederick Locker that the "London Lyrics" were "overrated"?

"I have suspected this," comments the poet, whose least noticeable characteristic was vanity; "but I was none the less sorry to hear him say so." Landor's reply to a lady who accused him of speaking of her with unkindness, "Madame, I have wasted my life in defending you!" was pardonable as a repartee. It was the exasperated utterance of self-defence; and there is a distinction to be drawn between the word which is flung without provocation, and the word which is the speaker's last resource. When "Bobus" Smith told Talleyrand that his mother had been a beautiful woman, and Talleyrand replied, "*C'était donc Monsieur votre père qui n'était pas bien*," we hold the witticism to have been cruel because unjustifiable. A man should be privileged to say his mother was beautiful, without inviting such a very obvious sarcasm. But when Madame de Staël pestered Talleyrand to say what he would do if he saw her and Madame Récamier drowning, the immortal answer, "*Madame de Staël sait tant de choses, que sans doute elle peut nager*," seems as kind as the circumstances warranted. "Corinne's" vanity was of the hungry type, which, crying perpetually for bread, was often fed with stones.

It has been well said that the difference between a man's habitual rudeness and habitual politeness is probably as great a difference as he will ever be able to make in the sum of human happiness; and the arithmetic of life consists in adding to, or subtracting from, the pleasurable moments of mortality. Neither is it worth while to draw fine distinctions between pleasure and happiness. If we are indifferent to the pleasures of our fellow creatures, it will not take us long to be indifferent to their happiness. We do not grow generous by ceasing to be considerate.

As a matter of fact, the perpetual surrender which politeness dictates cuts down to a reasonable figure the sum total of our selfishness. To listen when we are bored, to talk when we are listless, to stand when we are tired, to praise when we are indifferent, to accept the companionship of a stupid acquaintance when we might, at the expense of politeness, escape to a clever friend, to endure with smiling composure the near presence of people who are distasteful to us, — these things, and many like them, brace the sinews of our souls. They set a fine and delicate standard for common intercourse. They discipline us for the good of the community.

We cannot ring the bells backward, blot out the Civil War, and exchange the speed of modern life for the slumberous dignity of the Golden Age, — an age whose gilding brightens as we leave it shimmering in the distance. But even under conditions which have the disadvantage of existing, the American is not without gentleness of speech and spirit.

He is not always in a hurry. He is not always elbowing his way, or quivering with ill-bred impatience. Turn to him for help in a crowd, and feel the bright sureness of his response. Watch him under ordinary conditions, and observe his large measure of forbearance with the social deficiencies of his neighbour. Like Steele, he deems it humanity to laugh at an indifferent jest, and he has thereby earned for himself the reputation of being readily diverted. If he lacks the urbanities which embellish conversation, he is correspondingly free from the brutalities which degrade it. If his instinct does not prompt him to say something agreeable, it saves him from being wantonly unkind. Plain truths may be salutary; but unworthy truths are those which are destitute of any spiritual quality, which are not noble in themselves, and which are not nobly spoken; which may be trusted to offend, and which have never been known to illuminate. It is not for such asperities that we have perfected through the ages the priceless gift of language, that we seek to meet one another in the pleasant comradeship of life.

The Mission of Humour

"Laughter is my object: 'tis a property
In man, essential to his reason."

THOMAS RANDOLPH, *The Muses' Looking-Glass.*

AMERICAN humour is the pride of American hearts. It is held to be our splendid national characteristic, which we flaunt in the faces of other nations, conceiving them to have been less favoured by Providence. Just as the most effective way to disparage an author or an acquaintance—and we have often occasion to disparage both—is to say that he lacks a sense of humour, so the most effective criticism we can pass upon a nation is to deny it this valuable quality. American critics have written the most charming things about the keenness of American speech, the breadth and insight of American drollery, the electric current in American veins; and we, reading these pleasant felicitations, are wont to thank God with greater fervour than the occasion demands that we are more merry and wise than our neighbours. Mr. Brander Matthews, for example, has told us that there are newspaper writers in New York who have cultivated a wit, "not unlike Voltaire's." He mistrusts this wit because he finds it "corroding and disintegrating"; but he makes the comparison with that casual assurance which is a feature of American criticism.

Indeed, our delight in our own humour has tempted us to overrate both its literary value and its corrective qualities. We are never so apt to lose our sense of proportion as when we consider those beloved writers whom we hold to be humourists because they have made us laugh. It may be conceded that, as a people, we have an abiding and somewhat disquieting sense of fun. We are nimble of speech, we are more prone to levity than to seriousness, we are able to recognize a vital truth when it is presented to us under the familiar aspect of a jest, and we habitually allow ourselves certain forms of exaggeration, accepting, perhaps unconsciously, Hazlitt's verdict: "Lying is a species of wit, and shows spirit and invention." It is true also that no adequate provision is made in this country for the defective but valuable class without humour, which in England is exceedingly well cared for. American letters, American journalism, and American speech are so coloured by pleasantries, so accentuated by ridicule, that the silent and stodgy men, who are apt to represent a nation's real strength, hardly know where to turn for a little saving dulness. A deep vein of irony runs through every grade of society, making it possible for us to laugh at our own bitter discomfiture, and to scoff with startling distinctness at the evils which we passively permit. Just as the French monarchy under

Louis the Fourteenth was wittily defined as despotism tempered by epigram, so the United States have been described as a free republic fettered by jokes, and the taunt conveys a half-truth which it is worth our while to consider.

Now there are many who affirm that the humourist's point of view is, on the whole, the fairest from which the world can be judged. It is equally remote from the misleading side-lights of the pessimist and from the wilful blindness of the optimist. It sees things with uncompromising clearness, but it judges of them with tolerance and good temper. Moreover, a sense of the ridiculous is a sound preservative of social virtues. It places a proper emphasis on the judgments of our associates, it saves us from pitfalls of vanity and self-assurance, it lays the basis of that propriety and decorum of conduct upon which is founded the charm of intercourse among equals. And what it does for us individually, it does for us collectively. Our national apprehension of a jest fosters whatever grace of modesty we have to show. We dare not inflate ourselves as superbly as we should like to do, because our genial countrymen stand ever ready to prick us into sudden collapse. "It is the laugh we enjoy at our own expense which betrays us to the rest of the world."

Perhaps we laugh too readily. Perhaps we are sometimes amused when we ought to be angry. Perhaps we jest when it is our plain duty to reform. Here lies the danger of our national light-mindedness, — for it is seldom light-heartedness; we are no whit more light-hearted than our neighbours. A carping English critic has declared that American humour consists in speaking of hideous things with levity; and while so harsh a charge is necessarily unjust, it makes clear one abiding difference between the nations. An Englishman never laughs — except officially in "Punch" — over any form of political degradation. He is not in the least amused by jobbery, by bad service, by broken pledges. The seamy side of civilized life is not to him a subject for sympathetic mirth. He can pity the stupidity which does not perceive that it is cheated and betrayed; but penetration allied to indifference awakens his wondering contempt. "If you think it amusing to be imposed on," an Englishwoman once said to me, "you need never be at a loss for a joke."

In good truth, we know what a man is like by the things he finds laughable, we gauge both his understanding and his culture by his sense of the becoming and of the absurd. If the capacity for laughter be one of the things which separates men from brutes, the quality of laughter draws a sharp dividing-line between the trained intelligence and the vacant mind. The humour of a race interprets the character of a race, and the mental condition of which laughter is the expression is something which it behooves the student of human nature and the student of national traits to understand very clearly.

Now our American humour is, on the whole, good-tempered and decent. It is scandalously irreverent (reverence is a quality which seems to have been left out of our composition); but it has neither the pitilessness of the Latin, nor the grossness of the Teuton jest. As Mr. Gilbert said of Sir Beerbohm Tree's "Hamlet," it is funny without being coarse. We have at our best the art of being amusing in an agreeable, almost an amiable, fashion; but then we have also the rare good fortune to be very easily amused. Think of the current jokes provided for our entertainment week by week, and day by day. Think of the comic supplement of our Sunday newspapers, designed for the refreshment of the feeble-minded, and calculated to blight the spirits of any ordinarily intelligent household. Think of the debilitated jests and stories which a time-honoured custom inserts at the back of some of our magazines. It seems to be the custom of happy American parents to report to editors the infantile prattle of their engaging little children, and the editors print it for the benefit of those who escape the infliction first-hand. There is a story, pleasant but piteous, of Voltaire's listening with what patience he could muster to a comedy which was being interpreted by its author. At a certain point the dramatist read, "At this the Chevalier laughed"; whereupon Voltaire murmured enviously, "How fortunate the Chevalier was!" I think of that story whenever I am struck afresh by the ease with which we are moved to mirth.

A painstaking German student, who has traced the history of humour back to its earliest foundations, is of the opinion that there are eleven original jokes known to the world, or rather that there are eleven original and basic situations which have given birth to the world's jokes; and that all the pleasantries with which we are daily entertained are variations of these eleven originals, traceable directly or indirectly to the same sources. There are times when we are disposed to think eleven too generous a computation, and there are less weary moments in which the inexhaustible supply of situations still suggests fresh possibilities of laughter. Granted that the ever fertile mother-in-law jest and the one about the talkative barber were venerable in the days of Plutarch; there are others more securely and more deservedly rooted in public esteem which are, by comparison, new. Christianity, for example, must be held responsible for the missionary and cannibal joke, of which we have grown weary unto death; but which nevertheless possesses astonishing vitality, and exhibits remarkable breadth of treatment. Sydney Smith did not disdain to honour it with a joyous and unclerical quatrain; and the agreeable author of "Rab and his Friends" has told us the story of his fragile little schoolmate whose mother had destined him for a missionary, "though goodness knows there was n't enough of him to go around among many heathen."

To Christianity is due also the somewhat ribald mirth which has clung for centuries about Saint Peter as gatekeeper of Heaven. We can trace this mirth back to the rude jests of the earliest miracle plays. We see these jests repeated over and over again in the folklore of Latin and Germanic nations. And if we open a comic journal to-day, there is more than a chance that we shall find Saint Peter, key in hand, uttering his time-honoured witticisms. This well-worn situation depends, as a rule, upon that common element of fun-making, the incongruous. Saint Peter invaded by air-ships. Saint Peter outwitting a squad of banner-flying suffragettes. Saint

Peter losing his saintly temper over the expansive philanthropy of millionaires. Now and then a bit of true satire, like Mr. Kipling's "Tomlinson," conveys its deeper lesson to humanity. A recently told French story describes a lady of good reputation, family, and estate, presenting herself fearlessly at the gates of Heaven. Saint Peter receives her politely, and leads her through a street filled with lofty and beautiful mansions, any one of which she thinks will satisfy her requirements; but, to her amazement, they pass them by. Next they come to more modest but still charming houses with which she feels she could be reasonably content; but again they pass them by. Finally they reach a small and mean dwelling in a small and mean thoroughfare. "This," says Saint Peter, "is your habitation." "This!" cries the indignant lady; "I could not possibly live in any place so shabby and inadequate." "I am sorry, madame," replies the saint urbanely;

"but we have done the best we could with the materials you furnished us."

There are no bounds to the loyalty with which mankind clings to a well-established jest, there is no limit to the number of times a tale will bear retelling. Occasionally we give it a fresh setting, adorn it with fresh accessories, and present it as new-born to the world; but this is only another indication of our affectionate tenacity. I have heard that caustic gibe of Queen Elizabeth's anent the bishop's lady and the bishop's wife (the Tudors had a biting wit of their own) retold at the expense of an excellent lady, the wife of a living American bishop; and the story of the girl who, professing religion, gave her ear-rings to a sister, because she knew they were taking *her* to Hell,—a story which dates from the early Wesleyan revivals in England,—I have heard located in Philadelphia, and assigned to one of Mr. Torrey's evangelistic services. We still resort, as in the days of Sheridan, to our memories for our jokes, and to our imaginations for our facts.

Moreover, we Americans have jests of our own, — poor things for the most part, but our own. They are current from the Atlantic to the Pacific, they appear with commendable regularity in our newspapers and comic journals, and they have become endeared to us by a lifetime of intimacy. The salient characteristics of our great cities, the accepted traditions of our mining-camps, the contrast between East and West, the still more familiar contrast between the torpor of Philadelphia and Brooklyn ("In the midst of life," says Mr. Oliver Herford, "we are — in Brooklyn") and the uneasy speed of New York, — these things furnish abundant material for everyday American humour. There is, for example, the encounter between the Boston girl and the Chicago girl, who, in real life, might often be taken for each other;

but who, in the American joke, are as sharply differentiated as the Esquimo and the Hottentot. And there is the little Boston boy who always wears spectacles, who is always named Waldo, and who makes some innocent remark about "Literary Ethics," or the "Conduct of Life." We have known this little boy too long to bear a parting from him. Indeed, the mere suggestion that all Bostonians are forever immersed in Emerson is one which gives unfailing delight to the receptive American mind. It is a poor community which cannot furnish its archaic jest for the diversion of its neighbours.

The finest example of our bulldog resoluteness in holding on to a comic situation, or what we conceive to be a comic situation, may be seen every year when the twenty-second of February draws near, and the shops of our great and grateful Republic break out into an irruption of little hatchets, by which curious insignia we have chosen to commemorate our first President. These toys, occasionally combined with sprigs of artificial cherries, are hailed with unflagging delight, and purchased with what appears to be patriotic fervour. I have seen letter-carriers and post-office clerks wearing little hatchets in their button-holes, as though they were party buttons, or temperance badges. It is our great national joke, which I presume gains point from the dignified and reticent character of General Washington, and from the fact that he would have been sincerely unhappy could he have foreseen the senile character of a jest, destined, through our love of absurdity, our careful cultivation of the inappropriate, to be linked forever with his name.

The easy exaggeration which is a distinctive feature of American humour, and about which so much has been said and written, has its counterpart in sober and truth-telling England, though we are always amazed when we find it there, and fall to wondering, as we never wonder at home, in what spirit it was received. There are two kinds of exaggeration; exaggeration of statement, which is a somewhat primitive form of humour, and exaggeration of phrase, which implies a dexterous misuse of language, a skilful juggling with words. Sir John Robinson gives, as an admirable instance of exaggeration of statement, the remark of an American in London that his dining-room ceiling was so low that he could not have anything for dinner but soles. Sir John thought this could have been said only by an American, only by one accustomed to have a joke swiftly catalogued as a joke, and suffered to pass. An English jester must always take into account the mental attitude which finds "Gulliver's Travels" "incredible." When Mr. Edward FitzGerald said that the church at Woodbridge was so damp that fungi grew about the communion rail, Woodbridge ladies offered an indignant denial. When Dr. Thompson, the witty master of Trinity, observed of an undergraduate that "all the time he could spare from the neglect of his duties he gave to the adornment of his person," the sarcasm made its slow way into print; whereupon an intelligent British reader wrote to the periodical which had printed it, and explained painstakingly that, inasmuch as it was not possible to spare time from the neglect of anything, the criticism was inaccurate.

Exaggeration of phrase, as well as the studied understatement which is an even more effective form of ridicule, seem natural products of American humour. They sound, wherever we hear them, familiar to our ears. It is hard to believe that an English barrister, and not a Texas ranchman, described Boston as a town where respectability stalked unchecked. Mazarin's plaintive reflection, "Nothing is so disagreeable as to be obscurely hanged," carries with it an echo of Wyoming or Arizona. Mr. Gilbert's analysis of Hamlet's mental disorder, —

> "Hamlet is idiotically sane,
> With lucid intervals of lunacy,"—

has the pure flavour of American wit, — a wit which finds its most audacious expression in burlesquing bitter things, and which misfits its words with diabolic ingenuity. To match these alien jests, which sound so like our own, we have the whispered warning of an American usher (also quoted by Sir John Robinson) who opened the door to a late comer at one of Mr. Matthew Arnold's lectures: "Will you please make as little noise as you can, sir. The audience is asleep"; and the comprehensive remark of a New England scholar and wit that he never wanted to do anything in his life, that he did not find it was expensive, unwholesome, or immoral. This last observation embraces the wisdom of the centuries.

Solomon would have endorsed it, and it is supremely quotable as expressing a common experience with very uncommon felicity.

When we leave the open field of exaggeration, that broad area which is our chosen territory, and seek for subtler qualities in American humour, we find here and there a witticism which, while admittedly our own, has in it an Old-World quality. The epigrammatic remark of a Boston woman that men get and forget, and women give and forgive, shows the fine, sharp finish of Sydney Smith or Sheridan. A Philadelphia woman's observation, that she knew there could be no marriages in Heaven, because — "Well, women were there no doubt in plenty, and some men; but not a man whom any woman would have," is strikingly French. The word of a New York broker, when Mr. Roosevelt sailed for Africa, "Wall Street expects every lion to do its duty!" equals in brevity and malice the keen-edged satire of Italy. No sharper thrust was ever made at prince or potentate.

The truth is that our love of a jest knows no limit and respects no law. The incongruities of an unequal civilization (we live in the land of contrasts) have accustomed us to absurdities, and reconciled us to ridicule. We rather like being satirized by our own countrymen. We are very kind and a little cruel to our humourists. We crown them with praise, we hold them to our hearts, we pay them any price they ask for their wares; but we insist upon their being funny all the time. Once a humourist, always a humourist, is our way of thinking; and we resent even a saving lapse into seriousness on the part of those who have had the good or the ill fortune to make us laugh.

England is equally obdurate in this regard. Her love of laughter has been consecrated by Oxford, — Oxford, the dignified refuge of English scholarship, which passed by a score of American scholars to bestow her honours on our great American joker. And because of this love of laughter, so desperate in a serious nation, English jesters have enjoyed the uneasy privileges of a court fool. Look at poor Hood. What he really loved was to wallow in the pathetic, — to write such harrowing verses as the "Bridge of Sighs," and the "Song of the Shirt" (which achieved the rare distinction of being printed — like the "Beggar's Petition" — on cotton handkerchiefs), and the "Lady's Dream." Every time he broke from his traces, he plunged into these morasses of melancholy; but he was always pulled out again, and reharnessed to his jokes. He would have liked to be funny occasionally and spontaneously, and it was the will of his master, the public, that he should be funny all the time, or starve. Lord Chesterfield wisely said that a man should live within his wit as well as within his income; but if Hood had lived within his wit — which might then have possessed a vital and lasting quality — he would have had no income. His rôle in life was like that of a dancing bear, which is held to commit a solecism every time it settles wearily down on the four legs nature gave it.

The same tyrannous demand hounded Mr. Eugene Field along his joke-strewn path. Chicago, struggling with vast and difficult problems, felt the need of laughter, and required of Mr. Field that he should make her laugh. He accepted the responsibility, and, as a reward, his memory is hallowed in the city he loved and derided. New York echoes this sentiment (New York echoes more than she proclaims; she confirms rather than initiates); and when Mr. Francis Wilson wrote some years ago a charming and enthusiastic paper for the "Century Magazine," he claimed that Mr. Field was so great a humourist as to be — what all great humourists are,—a moralist as well. But he had little to quote which could be received as evidence in a court of criticism; and many of the paragraphs which he deemed it worth while to reprint were melancholy instances of that jaded wit, that exhausted vitality, which in no wise represented Mr. Field's mirth-loving spirit, but only the things which were ground out of him when he was not in a mirthful mood.

The truth is that humour as a lucrative profession is a purely modern device, and one which is much to be deplored. The older humourists knew the value of light and shade. Their fun was precious in proportion to its parsimony. The essence of humour is that it should be unexpected, that it should embody an element of surprise, that it should startle us out of that reasonable gravity which, after all, must be our habitual frame of mind. But the professional humourist cannot afford to be unexpected. The exigencies of his vocation compel him to be relentlessly droll from his first page to his last, and this accumulated drollery weighs like lead. Compared to it, sermons are as thistle-down, and political economy is gay.

It is hard to estimate the value of humour as a national trait. Life has its appropriate levities, its comedy side. We cannot "see it clearly and see it whole," without recognizing a great many absurdities which ought to be laughed at, a great deal of nonsense which is a fair target for ridicule. The heaviest charge brought against American humour is that it never keeps its target well in view. We laugh, but we are not purged by laughter of our follies; we jest, but our jests are apt to have a kitten's sportive irresponsibility. The lawyer offers a witticism in place of an argument, the diner-out tells an amusing story in lieu of conversation. Even the clergyman does not disdain a joke, heedless of Dr. Johnson's warning which should save him from that pitfall. Smartness furnishes sufficient excuse for the impertinence of children, and with purposeless satire the daily papers deride the highest dignitaries of the land.

Yet while always to be reckoned with in life and letters, American humour is not a powerful and consistent factor either for destruction or for reform. It lacks, for the most part, a logical basis, and the dignity of a supreme aim. Molière's humour amounted to a philosophy of life. He was wont to say that it was a difficult task to make gentlefolk laugh; but he succeeded in making them laugh at that which was laughable in themselves. He aimed his shafts at the fallacies and the duplicities which his countrymen ardently cherished, and he scorned the cheaper wit which contents itself with mocking at idols already discredited. As a result, he purged society, not of the follies that consumed it, but of the illusion that these follies were noble, graceful, and wise. "We do not plough or sow for fools," says a Russian proverb, "they grow of themselves"; but humour has accomplished a mighty work if it helps us to see that a fool is a fool, and not a prophet in the market-place. And if the man in the market-place chances to be a prophet, his message is safe from assault. No laughter can silence him, no ridicule weaken his words.

Carlyle's grim humour was also drilled into efficacy. He used it in orderly fashion; he gave it force by a stern principle of repression. He had (what wise man has not?) an honest respect for dulness, knowing that a strong and free people argues best — as Mr. Bagehot puts it — "in platoons." He had some measure of mercy for folly. But against the whole complicated business of pretence, against the pious, and respectable, and patriotic hypocrisies of a successful civilization, he hurled his taunts with such true aim that it is not too much to say there has been less real comfort and safety in lying ever since.

These are victories worth recording, and there is a big battlefield for American humour when it finds itself ready for the fray, when it leaves off firing squibs, and settles down to a compelling cannonade, when it aims less at the superficial incongruities of life, and more at the deep-rooted delusions which rob us of fair fame. It has done its best work in the field of political satire, where the "Biglow Papers" hit hard in their day, where Nast's cartoons helped to overthrow the Tweed dynasty, and where the indolent and luminous genius of Mr. Dooley has widened our mental horizon. Mr. Dooley is a philosopher, but his is the philosophy of the looker-on, of that genuine unconcern which finds Saint George and the dragon to be both a trifle ridiculous. He is always undisturbed, always illuminating, and not infrequently amusing; but he anticipates the smiling indifference with which those who come after us will look back upon our enthusiasms and absurdities. Humour, as he sees it, is that thrice blessed quality which enables us to laugh, when otherwise we should be in danger of weeping. "We are ridiculous animals," observes Horace Walpole unsympathetically, "and if angels have any fun in their hearts, how we must divert them."

It is this clear-sighted, non-combative humour which Americans love and prize, and the absence of which they reckon a heavy loss. Nor do they always ask, "a loss to whom?" Charles Lamb said it was no misfortune for a man to have a sulky temper. It was his friends who were unfortunate. And so with the man who has no sense of humour. He gets along very well without it. He is not aware that anything is lacking. He is not mourning his lot. What loss there is, his friends and neighbours bear. A man destitute of humour is apt to be a formidable person, not subject to sudden deviations from his chosen path, and incapable of frittering away his elementary forces by pottering over both sides of a question. He is often to be respected, sometimes to be feared, and always — if possible — to be avoided. His are the qualities which distance enables us to recognize and value at their worth. He fills his place in the scheme of creation; but it is for us to see that his place is not next to ours at table, where his unresponsiveness narrows the conversational area, and dulls the contagious ardour of speech. He may add to the wisdom of the ages, but he lessens the gayety of life.

Goodness and Gayety

"Can surly Virtue hope to find a friend?"—DR. JOHNSON.

SIR LESLIE STEPHEN has recorded his conviction that a sense of humour, being irreconcilable with some of the cardinal virtues, is lacking in most good men. Father Faber asserted, on the contrary, that a sense of humour is a great help in the religious life, and emphasized this somewhat unusual point of view with the decisive statement: "Perhaps nature does not contribute a greater help to grace than this."

Here are conflicting verdicts to be well considered. Sir Leslie Stephen knew more about humour than did Father Faber; Father Faber knew more about "grace" than did Sir Leslie Stephen; and both disputants were widely acquainted with their fellow men. Sir Leslie Stephen had a pretty wit of his own, but it may have lacked the qualities which make for holiness. There was in it the element of denial. He seldom entered the shrine where we worship our ideals in secret. He stood outside, remarks Mr. Birrell cheerily, "with a pail of cold water." Father Faber also possessed a vein of irony which was the outcome of a priestly experience with the cherished foibles of the world. He entered unbidden into the shrine where we worship our illusions in secret, and chilled us with unwelcome truths. I know of no harder experience than this. It takes time and trouble to persuade ourselves that the things we want to do are the things we ought to do. We balance our spiritual accounts with care. We insert glib phrases about duty into all our reckonings. There is nothing, or next to nothing, which cannot, if adroitly catalogued, be considered a duty; and it is this delicate mental adjustment which is disturbed by Father Faber's ridicule. "Self-deceit," he caustically observes, "seems to thrive on prayer, and to grow fat on contemplation."

If a sense of humour forces us to be candid with ourselves, then it can be reconciled, not only with the cardinal virtues — which are but a chilly quartette — but with the flaming charities which have consumed the souls of saints. The true humourist, objects Sir Leslie Stephen, sees the world as a tragi-comedy, a Vanity Fair, in which enthusiasm is out of place. But if the true humourist also sees himself presiding, in the sacred name of duty, over a booth in Vanity Fair, he may yet reach perfection. What Father Faber opposed so strenuously were, not the vanities of the profane, of the openly and cheerfully unregenerate; but the vanities of a devout and fashionable congregation, making especial terms — by virtue of its exalted station — with

Providence. These were the people whom he regarded all his priestly life with whimsical dismay. "Their voluntary social arrangements," he wrote in "Spiritual Conferences," "are the tyranny of circumstance, claiming our tenderest pity, and to be managed like the work of a Xavier, or a Vincent of Paul, which hardly left the saints time to pray. Their sheer worldliness is to be considered as an interior trial, with all manner of cloudy grand things to be said about it. They must avoid uneasiness, for such great graces as theirs can grow only in calmness and tranquillity."

This is irony rather than humour, but it implies a capacity to see the tragi-comedy of the world, without necessarily losing the power of enthusiasm. It also explains why Father Faber regarded an honest sense of the ridiculous as a help to goodness. The man or woman who is impervious to the absurd cannot well be stripped of self-delusion. For him, for her, there is no shaft which wounds. The admirable advice of Thomas à Kempis to keep away from people whom we desire to please, and the quiet perfection of his warning to the censorious, "In judging others, a man toileth in vain; for the most part he is mistaken, and he easily sinneth; but in judging and scrutinizing himself, he always laboureth with profit," can make their just appeal only to the humorous sense. So, too, the counsel of Saint Francis de Sales to the nuns who wanted to go barefooted, "Keep your shoes and change your brains"; the cautious query of Pope Gregory the First, concerning John the Faster, "Does he abstain even from the truth?" Cardinal Newman's axiom, "It is never worth while to call whity-brown white, for the sake of avoiding scandal"; and Father Faber's own felicitous comment on religious "hedgers," "A moderation which consists in taking immoderate liberties with God is hardly what the Fathers of the Desert meant when they preached their crusade in favour of discretion"; — are all spoken to those hardy and humorous souls who can bear to be honest with themselves.

The ardent reformer, intolerant of the ordinary processes of life, the ardent philanthropist, intolerant of an imperfect civilization, the ardent zealot, intolerant of man's unspiritual nature, are seldom disposed to gayety. A noble impatience of spirit inclines them to anger or to sadness. John Wesley, reformer, philanthropist, zealot, and surpassingly great in all three characters, strangled within his own breast the simple desire to be gay. He was a young man when he formed the resolution, "to labour after continual seriousness, not willingly indulging myself in the least levity of behaviour, or in laughter, — no, not for a moment"; and for more than fifty years he kept — probably with no great difficulty — this stern resolve. The mediæval saying, that laughter has sin for a father and folly for a mother, would have meant to Wesley more than a figure of speech. Nothing could rob him of a dry and bitter humour ("They won't let me go to Bedlam," he wrote, "because they say I make the inmates mad, nor into Newgate, because I make them wicked"); but there was little in his creed or in the scenes of his labours to promote cheerfulness of spirit.

This disciplining of nature, honest, erring human nature, which could, if permitted, make out a fair case for itself, is not an essential element of the evangelist's code. In the hands of men less great than Wesley, it has been known to nullify the work of a lifetime. The Lincolnshire farmer who, after listening to a sermon on Hell, said to his wife, "Noä, Sally, it woänt do. Noä constitootion could stand it," expressed in his own fashion the healthy limit of endurance. Our spiritual constitutions break under a pitiless strain. When we read in the diary of Henry Alline, quoted by Dr. William James in his "Varieties of Religious Experience," "On Wednesday the twelfth I preached at a wedding, and had the happiness thereby to be the means of excluding carnal mirth," we are not merely sorry for the wedding guests, but beset by doubts as to their moral gain.

Why should Henry Martyn, that fervent young missionary who gave his life for his cause with the straight-forward simplicity of a soldier, have regretted so bitterly an occasional lapse into good spirits? He was inhumanly serious, and he prayed by night and day to be saved from his "besetting sin" of levity. He was consumed by the flame of religious zeal, and he bewailed at grievous length, in his diary, his "light, worldly spirit." He toiled unrestingly, taking no heed of his own physical weakness, and he asked himself (when he had a minute to spare) what would become of his soul, should he be struck dead in a "careless mood." We have Mr. Birrell's word for it that once, in an old book about India, he came across an after-dinner jest of Henry Martyn's; but the idea was so incongruous that the startled essayist was disposed to doubt the evidence of his senses. "There must have been a mistake somewhere."

To such a man the world is not, and never can be, a tragi-comedy, and laughter seems forever out of place. When a Madeira negress, a good Christian after her benighted fashion, asked Martyn if the English were ever baptized, he did not think the innocent question funny, he thought it horrible. He found Saint Basil's writings unsatisfactory, as lacking "evangelical truth"; and, could he have heard this great doctor of the Church fling back a witticism in the court of an angry magistrate, he would probably have felt more doubtful than ever concerning the status of the early

Fathers. It is a relief to turn from the letters of Martyn, with their aloofness from the cheerful currents of earth, to the letters of Bishop Heber, who, albeit a missionary and a keen one, had always a laugh for the absurdities which beset his wandering life. He could even tell with relish the story of the drunken pedlar whom he met in Wales, and who confided to him that, having sold all his wares, he was trying to drink up the proceeds before he got home, lest his wife should take the money away from him. Heber, using the argument which he felt would be of most avail, tried to frighten the man into soberness by picturing his wife's wrath ; whereupon the adroit scamp replied that he knew what *that* would be, and had taken the precaution to have his hair cut short, so that she could not get a grip on it. Martyn could no more have chuckled over this depravity than he could have chuckled over the fallen angels ; but Saint Teresa could have laughed outright, her wonderful, merry, infectious laugh; and have then proceeded to plead, to scold, to threaten, to persuade, until a chastened and repentant pedlar, money in hand, and some dim promptings to goodness tugging at his heart, would have tramped bravely and soberly home.

It is so much the custom to obliterate from religious memoirs all vigorous human traits, all incidents which do not tend to edification, and all contemporary criticism which cannot be smoothed into praise, that what is left seems to the disheartened reader only a pale shadow of life. It is hard to make any biography illustrate a theme, or prove an argument; and the process by which such results are obtained is so artificial as to be open to the charge of untruth. Because General Havelock was a good Baptist as well as a good soldier, because he expressed a belief in the efficacy of prayer (like Cromwell's "Trust in God, and keep your powder dry"), and because he wrote to his wife, when sent to the relief of Lucknow, "May God give me wisdom and strength for the work!"—which, after all, was a natural enough thing for any man to say,—he was made the subject of a memoir determinedly and depressingly devout, in which his family letters were annotated as though they were the epistles of Saint Paul. Yet this was the man who, when Lucknow *was* relieved, behaved as if nothing out of the ordinary had happened to besiegers or besieged. "He shook hands with me," wrote Lady Inglis in her journal, "and observed that he feared we had suffered a great deal." That was all. He might have said as much had the little garrison been incommoded by a spell of unusual heat, or by an epidemic of measles.

As a matter of fact, piety is a by no means uncommon attribute of soldiers, and there was no need on the part of the Reverend Mr. Brock, who compiled these shadowy pages, to write as though General Havelock had been a rare species of the genius military. We know that what the English Puritans especially resented in Prince Rupert was his insistence on regimental prayers. They could pardon his raids, his breathless charges, his bewildering habit of appearing where he was least expected or desired; but that he should usurp their own especial prerogative of piety was more than they could bear. It is probable that Rupert's own private petitions resembled the memorable prayer offered by Sir Jacob Astley (a hardy old Cavalier who was both devout and humorous) before the battle of Edgehill: "Oh, Lord, Thou knowest how busy I must be this day. If I forget Thee, do not Thou forget me. March on, boys!"

If it were not for a few illuminating anecdotes, and the thrice blessed custom of letter writing, we should never know what manner of thing human goodness, exalted human goodness, is; and so acquiesce ignorantly in Sir Leslie Stephen's judgment. The sinners of the world stand out clear and distinct, full of vitality, and of an engaging candour. The saints of Heaven shine dimly through a nebulous haze of hagiology. They are embodiments of inaccessible virtues, as remote from us and from our neighbours as if they had lived on another planet. There is no more use in asking us to imitate these incomprehensible creatures than there would be in asking us to climb by easy stages to the moon. Without some common denominator, sinner and saint are as aloof from each other as sinner and archangel. Without some clue to the saint's spiritual identity, the record of his labours and hardships, fasts, visions, and miracles, offers nothing more helpful than bewilderment. We may be edified or we may be sceptical, according to our temperament and training;

but a profound unconcern devitalizes both scepticism and edification. What have we mortals in common with these perfected prodigies of grace?

It was Cardinal Newman who first entered a protest against "minced" saints, against the pious and popular custom of chopping up human records into lessons for the devout. He took exception to the hagiological licence which assigns lofty motives to trivial actions. "The saint from humility made no reply." "The saint was silent out of compassion for the ignorance of the speaker." He invited us to approach the Fathers of the Church in their unguarded moments, in their ordinary avocations, in their moods of gayety and depression; and, when we accepted the invitation, these figures, lofty and remote, became imbued with life. It is one thing to know that Saint Chrysostom retired at twenty-three to a monastery near Antioch, and there spent six years in seclusion and study. It is another and more enlightening thing to be made aware, through the medium of his own letters, that he took this step with reasonable doubts and misgivings, — doubts which extended to the freshness of the monastery bread, misgivings which concerned themselves with the sweetness of the monastery oil. And when we read these candid expressions of anxiety, Saint Chrysostom, by virtue of his healthy young appetite, and his distaste (which any poor sinner can share) for rancid oil, becomes a man and a brother. It is yet more consoling to know that when well advanced in sainthood, when old, austere, exiled, and suffering many privations for conscience' sake, Chrysostom was still disposed to be a trifle fastidious about his bread. He writes from Cæsarea to Theodora that he has at last found clean water to drink, and bread which can be chewed. "Moreover, I no longer wash myself in broken crockery, but have contrived some sort of bath; also I have a bed to which I can confine myself."

If Saint Chrysostom possessed, according to Newman, a cheerful temper, and "a sunniness of mind all his own," Saint Gregory of Nazianzus was a fair humourist, and Saint Basil was a wit. "Pensive playfulness" is Newman's phrase for Basil, but there was a speed about his retorts which did not always savour of pensiveness. When the furious governor of Pontus threatened to tear out his liver, Basil, a confirmed invalid, replied suavely, "It is a kind intention. My liver, as at present located, has given me nothing but uneasiness."

To Gregory, Basil was not only guide, philosopher, and friend; but also a cherished target for his jests. It has been wisely said that we cannot really love anybody at whom we never laugh. Gregory loved Basil, revered him, and laughed at him. Does Basil complain, not unnaturally, that Tiberina is cold, damp, and muddy, Gregory writes to him unsympathetically that he is a "clean-footed, tip-toeing, capering man." Does Basil promise a visit, Gregory sends word to Amphilochus that he must have some fine pot-herbs, "lest Basil should be hungry and cross." Does Gregory visit Basil in his solitude at Pontus, he expresses in no measured terms his sense of the discomfort he endures. It would be hard to find, in all the annals of correspondence, a letter written with a more laudable and well-defined intention of teasing its recipient, than the one dispatched to Basil by Gregory after he has made good his escape from the austerities of his friend's housekeeping.

"I have remembrance of the bread and of the broth, — so they were named, — and shall remember them; how my teeth stuck in your hunches, and lifted and heaved themselves as out of paste. You, indeed, will set it out in tragic style, taking a sublime tone from your own sufferings; but for me, unless that true Lady Bountiful, your mother, had rescued me quickly, showing herself in my need like a haven to the tempest-tossed, I had been dead long ago, getting myself little honour, though much pity, from Pontic hospitality."

This is not precisely the tone in which the lives of the saints (of any saints of any creeds) are written. Therefore is it better to read what the saints say for themselves than what has been said about them. This is not precisely the point of view which is presented unctuously for our consideration, yet it makes all other points of view intelligible. It is contrary to human nature to court privations. We know that the saints did court them, and valued them as avenues to grace. It is in accord with human nature to meet privations cheerfully, and with a whimsical sense of discomfiture. When we hear the echo of a saint's laughter ringing down the centuries, we have a clue to his identity; not to his whole and heroic self, but to that portion of him which we can best understand, and with which we claim some humble brotherhood. We ourselves are not hunting assiduously for hardships; but which one of us has not summoned up courage enough to laugh in the face of disaster?

There is no reading less conducive to good spirits than the recitals of missionaries, or than such pitiless records as those compiled by Dr. Thomas William Marshall in his two portly volumes on "Christian Missions." The heathen, as portrayed by Dr. Marshall, do not in the least resemble the heathen made familiar to us by the hymns and tracts of our infancy. So far from calling on us to deliver their land "from error's chain," they mete out prompt and cruel death to their deliverers. So far from thirsting for Gospel truths, they thirst for the blood of the intruders. This is frankly discouraging, and we could never read so many pages of disagreeable happenings, were it not for the gayety of the letters which Dr. Marshall quotes, and which deal less in heroics than in pleasantries. Such men as Bishop Berneux, the Abbé Rétord, and Father Féron, missionaries in Cochin-China and Corea, all possessed that protective sense of humour which kept up their spirits and their enthusiasms. Father Féron, for example, hidden away in the "Valley of the Pines," six hundred miles from safety, writes to his sister in the autumn of 1858: —

"I am lodged in one of the finest houses in the village, that of the catechist, an opulent man. It is considered to be worth a pound sterling. Do not laugh; there are some of the value of eightpence. My room has a sheet of paper for a door, the rain filters through my grass-covered roof as fast as it falls outside, and two large kettles barely suffice to receive it. . . . The Prophet Elisha, at the house of the Shunamite, had for furniture a bed, a table, a chair, and a candlestick, — four pieces in all. No superfluity there. Now if I search well, I can also find four articles in my room; a wooden candlestick, a trunk, a pair of shoes, and a pipe. Bed none, chairs none, table none. Am I, then, richer or poorer than the Prophet? It is not an easy question to answer, for, granting that his quarters were more comfortable than mine, yet none of the things belonged to him; while in my case, although the candlestick is borrowed from the chapel, and the trunk from Monseigneur Berneux, the shoes (worn only when I say Mass) and the pipe are my very own."

Surely if one chanced to be the sister of a missionary in Corea, and apprehensive, with good cause, of his personal safety, this is the kind of a letter one would be glad to receive. The comfort of finding one's brother disinclined to take what Saint Gregory calls "a sublime tone" would tend — illogically, I own, — to ease the burden of anxiety. Even the remote reader, sick of discouraging details, experiences a renewal of confidence, and all because Father Féron's good humour is of the common kind which we can best understand, and with which it befits every one of us to meet the vicissitudes of life.

I have said that the ardent reformer is seldom gay. Small wonder, when his eyes are turned upon the dark places of earth, and his whole strength is consumed in combat. Yet Saint Teresa, the most redoubtable reformer of her day, was gay. No other word expresses the quality of her gladness. She was not only spiritually serene, she was humanly gay, and this in the face of acute ill-health, and many profound discouragements. We have the evidence of all her contemporaries, — friends, nuns, patrons, and confessors; and we have the far more enduring testimony of her letters, in proof of this mirthfulness of spirit, which won its way into hearts, and lightened the austerities of her rule. "A very cheerful and gentle disposition, an excellent temper, and absolutely void of melancholy," wrote Ribera. "So merry that when she laughed, every one laughed with her, but very grave when she was serious."

There is a strain of humour, a delicate and somewhat biting wit in the correspondence of Saint Teresa, and in her admonitions to her nuns. There is also an inspired common sense which we hardly expect to find in the writings of a religious and a mystic. But Teresa was not withdrawn from the world. She travelled incessantly from one end of Spain to the other, establishing new foundations, visiting her convents, and dealing with all classes of men, from the soldier to the priest, from the prince to the peasant. The severity of her discipline was tempered by a tolerant and half-amused insight into the pardonable foibles of humanity. She held back her nuns with one hand from "the frenzy of self-mortification," which is the mainstay of spiritual vanity, and with the other hand from a too solicitous regard for their own comfort and convenience. They were not to consider that the fear of a headache, — a non-existent headache threatening the future — was sufficient excuse for absenting themselves from choir; and, if they were too ailing to practise any other austerities, the rule of silence, she reminded them, could do the feeblest no harm. "Do not contend wordily over matters of no consequence," was her counsel of perfection. "Fly a thousand leagues from such observations as 'You see I was right,' or 'They did me an injustice.'"

Small wonder that peace reigned among the discalced Carmelites so long as Teresa ruled. Practical and fearless (save when a lizard ran up her sleeve, on which occasion she confesses she nearly "died of fright,") her much-sought advice was always on the side of reason. Asceticism she prized; dirt she abhorred. "For the love of Heaven," she wrote to the Provincial, Gratian, then occupied with his first foundation of discalced friars, "let your fraternity be careful that they have clean beds and tablecloths, even though it be more expensive, for it is a terrible thing not to be cleanly." No persuasion could induce her to retain a novice whom she believed to be unfitted for her rule: — "We women are not so easy to know," was her scornful reply to the Jesuit, Olea, who held his judgment in such matters to be infallible; but nevertheless her practical soul yearned over a well-dowered nun. When an "excellent novice" with a fortune of six thousand ducats presented herself at the gates of the poverty-stricken convent in Seville, Teresa, then in Avila, was consumed with anxiety lest such an acquisition should, through some blunder, be lost. "For the love of God," wrote the wise old saint to the prioress in Seville, "if she enters, bear with a few defects, for well does she deserve it."

This is not the type of anecdote which looms large in the volumes of "minced saints" prepared for pious readers, and its absence has accustomed us to dissever humour from sanctity. But a candid soul is, as a rule, a humorous soul, awake to the tragi-comic aspect of life, and immaculately free from self-deception. And to such souls, cast like Teresa's in heroic mould, comes the perception of great moral truths, together with the sturdy strength which supports enthusiasm in the face of human disabilities. They are the lantern-bearers of every age, of every race, of every creed, *les âmes bien nées* whom it behooves us to approach fearlessly out of the darkness, for so only can we hope to understand.

The Nervous Strain

"Which fiddle-strings is weakness to expredge my nerves this night." — MRS. GAMP.

ANNA ROBESON BURR, in her scholarly analysis of the world's great autobiographies, has found occasion to compare the sufferings of the American woman under the average conditions of life with the endurance of the woman who, three hundred years ago, confronted dire vicissitudes with something closely akin to insensibility. "Today," says Mrs. Burr, "a child's illness, an over-gay season, the loss of an investment, a family jar, — these are accepted as sufficient cause for over-strained nerves and temporary retirement to a sanitarium. *Then*, war, rapine, fire, sword, prolonged and mortal peril, were considered as furnishing no excuse to men or women for altering the habits, or slackening the energies, of their daily existence."

As a matter of fact, Isabella d' Este witnessed the sacking of Rome without so much as thinking of nervous prostration. This was nearly four hundred years ago, but it is the high-water mark of feminine fortitude. To live through such days and nights of horror, and emerge therefrom with unimpaired vitality, and unquenched love for a beautiful and dangerous world, is to rob the words "shock" and "strain" of all dignity and meaning. To resume at once the interrupted duties and pleasures of life was, for the Marchioness of Mantua, obligatory; but none the less we marvel that she could play her rôle so well.

A hundred and thirty years later, Sir Ralph Verney, an exiled royalist, sent his young wife back to England to petition Parliament for the restoration of his sequestrated estates. Lady Verney's path was beset by difficulties and dangers. She had few friends and many enemies, little money and cruel cares. She was, it is needless to state, pregnant when she left France, and paused in her work long enough to bear her husband "a lusty boy"; after which Sir Ralph writes that he fears she is neglecting her guitar, and urges her to practise some new music before she returns to the Continent.

Such pages of history make tonic reading for comfortable ladies who, in their comfortable homes, are bidden by their comfortable doctors to avoid the strain of anything and everything which makes the game of life worth living. It is our wont to think of our great-great-great-grandmothers as spending their days in undisturbed tranquillity. We take imaginary naps in their quiet rooms, envying the serenity of an existence unvexed by telegrams, telephones, clubs, lectures, committee-meetings, suffrage demonstrations, and societies for harrying our neighbours. How sweet and still those spacious rooms must have been! What was the remote tinkling of a harp, compared to pianolas, and phonographs, and all the infernal contrivances of science for producing and perpetuating noise? What was a fear of ghosts compared to a knowledge of germs? What was repeated child-bearing, or occasional smallpox, compared to the "over-pressure" upon "delicate organisms," which is making the fortunes of doctors to-day?

So we argue. Yet in good truth our ancestors had their share of pressure, and more than their share of ill-health. The stomach was the same ungrateful and rebellious organ then that it is now. Nature was the same strict accountant then that she is now, and balanced her debit and credit columns with the same relentless accuracy. The "liver" of the last century has become, we are told, the "nerves" of to-day; which transmigration should be a bond of sympathy between the new woman and that unchangeable article, man. We have warmer spirits and a higher vitality than our home-keeping great-grandmothers ever had. We are seldom hysterical, and we never faint. If we are gay, our gayeties involve less exposure and fatigue. If we are serious-minded, our attitude towards our own errors is one of unaffected leniency. That active, lively, all-embracing assurance of eternal damnation, which was part of John Wesley's vigorous creed, might have broken down the nervous system of a mollusk. The modern nurse, jealously guarding her patient from all but the neutralities of life, may be pleased to know that when Wesley made his memorable voyage to Savannah, a young woman on board the ship gave birth to her first child; and Wesley's journal is full of deep concern, because the other women about her failed to improve the occasion by exhorting the poor tormented creature "to fear Him who is able to inflict sharper pains than these."

As for the industrious idleness which is held to blame for the wrecking of our nervous systems, it was not unknown to an earlier generation. Madame Le Brun assures us that, in her youth, pleasure-loving people would leave Brussels early in the morning, travel all day to Paris, to hear the opera, and travel all night home. "That," she observes, — as well she may, — "was considered being fond of the opera." A paragraph in one of Horace Walpole's letters gives us the record of a day and a night in the life of an English lady, — sixteen hours of "strain" which would put New York to the blush. "I heard the Duchess of Gordon's journal of last Monday," he writes to Miss Berry in the spring of 1791. "She first went to hear Handel's music in the Abbey; she then clambered over the benches, and went to Hastings's trial in the Hall; after dinner, to the play; then to Lady Lucan's assembly; after that to Ranelagh, and returned to Mrs. Hobart's faro-table; gave a ball herself in the evening of that morning, into which she must have got a good way; and set out for Scotland the next day. Hercules could not have accomplished a quarter of her labours in the same space of time."

Human happiness was not to this gay Gordon a "painless languor"; and if she failed to have nervous prostration — under another name — she was cheated of her dues. Wear-and-tear plus luxury is said to break down the human system more rapidly than wear-and-tear plus want; but perhaps wear-and-tear plus pensive self-consideration is the most destructive agent of all. "Après tout, c'est un monde passable"; and the Duchess of Gordon was too busy acquainting herself with this fact to count the costs, or even pay the penalty.

One thing is sure, — we cannot live in the world without vexation and without fatigue. We are bidden to avoid both, just as we are bidden to avoid an injudicious meal, a restless night, a close and crowded room, an uncomfortable sensation of any kind, — as if these things were not the small coin of existence. An American doctor who was delicately swathing his nervous patient in cotton wool, explained that, as part of the process, she must be secluded from everything unpleasant. No disturbing news must be told her. No needless contradiction must be offered her. No disagreeable word must be spoken to her. "But doctor," said the lady, who had long before retired with her nerves from all lively contact with realities, "who is there that would dream of saying anything disagreeable to me?" "Madam," retorted the physician, irritated for once into unprofessional candour, "have you then no family?"

There *is* a bracing quality about family criticism, if we are strong enough to bear its veracities. What makes it so useful is that it recognizes existing conditions. All the well-meant wisdom of the "Don't Worry" books is based upon immunity from common sensations and from every-day experience. We must — unless we are insensate — take our share of worry along with our share of mishaps. All the kindly counsellors who, in scientific journals, entreat us to keep on tap "a vivid hope, a cheerful resolve, an absorbing interest," by way of nerve-tonic, forget that these remedies do not grow under glass. They are hardy plants, springing naturally in eager and animated natures. Artificial remedies might be efficacious in an artificial world. In a real world, the best we can do is to meet the plagues of life as Dick Turpin met the hangman's noose, "with manly resignation, though with considerable disgust." Moreover, disagreeable things are often very stimulating. A visit to some beautiful little rural almshouses in England convinced me that what kept the old inmates alert and in love with life was, not the charm of their bright-coloured gardens, nor the comfort of their cottage hearths, but the vital jealousies and animosities which pricked their sluggish blood to tingling.

There are prophets who predict the downfall of the human race through undue mental development, who foresee us (flatteringly, I must say) winding up the world's history in a kind of intellectual apotheosis. They write distressing pages about the strain of study in schools, the strain of examinations, the strain of competition, the strain of night-work, when children ought to be in bed, the strain of day-work, when they ought to be at play. An article on "Nerves and Over-Pressure" in the "Dublin Review" conveys the impression that little boys and girls are dangerously absorbed in their lessons, and draws a fearful picture of these poor innocents literally "grinding from babyhood." It is over-study (an evil from which our remote ancestors were wholly and happily exempt) which lays, so we are told, the foundation of all our nervous disorders. It is this wasting ambition which exhausts the spring of childhood and the vitality of youth.

There must be some foundation for fears so often expressed; though when we look at the blooming boys and girls of our acquaintance, with their placid ignorance and their love of fun, their glory in athletics and their transparent contempt for learning, it is hard to believe that they are breaking down their constitutions by study. Nor is it possible to acquire even the most modest substitute for education without some effort. The carefully fostered theory that school-work can be made easy and enjoyable breaks down as soon as anything, however trivial, has to be learned.

Life is a real thing in the school-room and in the nursery; and children — left to their own devices — accept it with wonderful courage and sagacity. If we allow to their souls some noble and free expansion, they may be trusted to divert themselves from that fretful self-consciousness which the nurse calls naughtiness, and the doctor, nerves. A little wholesome neglect, a little discipline, plenty of play, and a fair chance to be glad and sorry as the hours swing by, — these things are not too much to grant to childhood. That careful coddling which deprives a child of all delicate and strong emotions lest it be saddened, or excited, or alarmed, leaves it dangerously soft of fibre. Coleridge, an unhappy little lad at school, was lifted out of his own troubles by an acquaintance with the heroic sorrows of the world. There is no page of history, however dark, there is no beautiful old tale, however tragic, which does not impart some strength and some distinction to the awakening mind. It is possible to overrate the superlative merits of insipidity as a mental and moral force in the development of youth.

There are people who surrender themselves without reserve to needless activities, who have a real affection for telephones, and district messengers, and the importunities of their daily mail. If they are women, they put special delivery stamps on letters which would lose nothing by a month's delay. If they are men, they exult in the thought that they can be reached by wireless telegraphy on mid-ocean. We are apt to think of these men and women as painful products of our own time and of our own land; but they have probably existed since the building of the Tower of Babel, — a nerve-racking piece of work which gave peculiar scope to strenuous and impotent energies.

A woman whose every action is hurried, whose every hour is open to disturbance, whose every breath is drawn with superfluous emphasis, will talk about the nervous strain under which she is living, as though dining out and paying the cook's wages were the things which are breaking her down. The remedy proposed for such "strain" is withdrawal from the healthy buffetings of life, — not for three days, as Burke withdrew in order that he might read "Evelina," and be rested and refreshed thereby; but long enough to permit of the notion that immunity from buffetings is a possible condition of existence, — of all errors, the most irretrievable.

It has been many centuries since Marcus Aurelius observed the fretful disquiet of Rome, which must have been strikingly like our fretful disquiet to-day, and proffered counsel, unheeded then as now: "Take pleasure in one thing and rest in it, passing from one social act to another, thinking of God."

The Girl Graduate

"When I find learning and wisdom united in one person, I do not wait to consider the sex; I bend in admiration." — LA BRUYÈRE.

WE shall never know, though we shall always wonder, why certain phrases, carelessly flung to us by poet or by orator, should be endowed with regrettable vitality. When Tennyson wrote that mocking line about "sweet girl graduates in their golden hair," he could hardly have surmised that it would be quoted exuberantly year after weary year, or that with each successive June it would reappear as the inspiration of flowery editorials, and of pictures, monotonously amorous, in our illustrated journals. Perhaps in view of the serious statistics which have for some time past girdled the woman student, statistics dealing exhaustively with her honours, her illnesses, her somewhat nebulous achievements, and the size of her infant families, it is as well to realize that the big, unlettered, easy-going world regards her still from the standpoint of golden hair, and of the undying charm of immaturity.

In justice to the girl graduate, it must be said that she takes herself simply and sanely. It is not her fault that statisticians note down every breath she draws; and many of their most heartrending allegations have passed into college jokes, traditional jokes, fated to descend from senior to freshman for happy years to come. The student learns in the give-and-take of communal life to laugh at many things, partly from sheer high spirits, partly from youthful cynicism, and the habit of sharpening her wit against her neighbour's. It is commonly believed that she is an unduly serious young person with an insatiable craving for knowledge; in reality she is often as healthily unresponsive as is her Yale or Harvard brother. If she cannot yet weave her modest acquirements into the tissue of her life as unconcernedly as her brother does, it is not because she has been educated beyond her mental capacity: it is because social conditions are not for her as inevitable as they are for him.

Things were simpler in the old days, when college meant for a woman the special training needed for a career; when, battling often with poverty, she made every sacrifice for the education which would give her work a market value; and when all she asked in return was the dignity of self-support. Now many girls, unspurred by necessity or by ambition, enter college because they are keen for personal and intellectual freedom, because they desire the activities and the pleasures which college generously gives. They bring with them some traditions of scholarship, and some knowledge of the world, with a corresponding elasticity of judgment. They may or may not be good students, but their influence makes for serenity and balance. Their four years' course lacks, however, a definite goal. It is a training for life, as is the four years' course of their Yale or Harvard brothers, but with this difference, — the college woman's life is still open to adjustment.

Often it adjusts itself along time-honoured lines, and with time-honoured results. In this happy event, some mystic figures are recalculated in scientific journals, the graduate's babies are added to the fractional birth-rate accredited to the college woman, her family and friends consider that, individually, she has settled the whole vexed question of education and domesticity, and the world, enamoured always of the traditional type of femininity, goes on its way rejoicing. If, however, the graduate evinces no inclination for social and domestic delights, if she longs to do some definite work, to breathe the breath of man's activities, and to guide herself, as a man must do, through the intricate mazes of life, it is the part of justice and of wisdom to let her try. Nothing steadies the restless soul like work, — real work which has an economic value, and is measured by the standards of the world. The college woman has been trained to independence of thought, and to a wide reasonableness of outlook. She has also received some equipment in the way of knowledge; not more, perhaps, than could be easily absorbed in the ordinary routine of life, but enough to give her a fair start in whatever field of industry she enters. If she develops into efficiency, if she makes good her hold upon work, she silences her critics. If she fails, and can, in Stevenson's noble words, "take honourable defeat to be a form of victory," she has not wasted her endeavours.

It is strange that the advantages of a college course for girls—advantages solid and reckonable—should be still so sharply questioned by men and women of the world. It is stranger still that its earnest advocates should claim for it in a special manner the few merits it does not possess. When President David Starr Jordan, of Leland Stanford University, tells us that "it is hardly necessary among intelligent men and women to argue that a good woman is a better one for having received a college education; anything short of this is inadequate for the demands of modern life and modern culture"; we can only echo the words of the wise cat in Mr. Froude's "Cat's Pilgrimage," "There may be truth in what you say, but your view is limited."

Goodness, indeed, is not a matter easily opened to discussion. Who can pigeonhole goodness, or assign it a locality? But culture (if by the word we mean that common understanding of the world's best traditions which enables us to meet one another with mental ease) is not the fair fruit of a college education. It is primarily a matter of inheritance, of lifelong surroundings, of temperament, of delicacy of taste, of early and vivid impressions. It is often found in college, but it is not a collegiate product. The steady and absorbing work demanded of a student who is seeking a degree, precludes wide wanderings "in the realms of gold." If, in her four years of study, she has gained some solid knowledge of one or two subjects, with a power of approach in other directions, she has done well, and justified the wisdom of the group system, which makes for intellectual discipline and real attainments.

In households where there is little education, the college daughter is reverenced for what she knows,—for her Latin, her mathematics, her biology. What she does not know, being also unknown to her family, causes no dismay. In households where the standard of cultivation is high, the college daughter is made the subject of good-humoured ridicule, because she lacks the general information of her sisters, — because she has never heard of Abelard and Héloïse, of Graham of Claverhouse, of "The Beggars' Opera." Nobody expects the college son to know these things, or is in the least surprised when he does not; but the college daughter is supposed to be the repository of universal erudition. Every now and then somebody rushes into print with indignant illustrations of her ignorance, as though ignorance were not the one common possession of mankind. Those of us who are not undergoing examinations are not driven to reveal it, — a comfortable circumstance, which need not, however, make us unreasonably proud.

Therefore, when we are told of sophomores who place Shakespeare in the twelfth, and Dickens in the seventeenth century, who are under the impression that "Don Quixote" flowed from the fertile pen of Mr. Marion Crawford, and who are not aware that a gentleman named James Boswell wrote a most entertaining life of another gentleman named Samuel Johnson, we need not lift up horror-stricken hands to Heaven, but call to mind how many other things there are in this world to know. That a girl student should mistake "*Launcelot Gobbo*" for King Arthur's knight is not a matter of surprise to one who remembers how three young men, graduates of the oldest and proudest colleges in the land, placidly confessed ignorance of "*Petruchio.*" Shakespeare, after all, belongs to "the realms of gold." The higher education, as now understood, permits the student to escape him, and to escape the Bible as well. As a consequence of these exemptions, a bachelor of arts may be, and often is, unable to meet his intellectual equals with mental ease. Allusions that have passed into the common vocabulary of cultivated men and women have no meaning for him. Does not Mr. Andrew Lang tell us of an Oxford student who wanted to know what people meant when they said "hankering after the flesh-pots of Egypt"; and has not the present writer been asked by a Harvard graduate if she could remember a Joseph, "somewhere" in the Old Testament, who was "decoyed into Egypt by a coat of many colours"?

To measure *any* form of schooling by its direct results is to narrow a wide issue to insignificance. The by-products of education are the things which count. It has been said by an admirable educator that the direct results obtained from Eton and Rugby are a few copies of indifferent Latin verse; the by-products are the young men who run the Indian Empire. We may be startled for a moment by discovering a student of political economy to be wholly and happily ignorant of Mr. Lloyd-George's "Budget," the most vivid object-lesson of our day; but how many Americans who talked about the budget, and had impassioned views on the subject, knew what it really contained? If the student's intelligence is so trained that she has some adequate grasp of economics, if she has been lifted once and forever out of the Robin Hood school of political economy, which is so dear to a woman's generous heart, it matters little how early or how late she becomes acquainted with the history of her own time. "Depend upon it," said the wise Dr. Johnson, whom undergraduates are sometimes wont to slight, "no woman was ever the worse for sense and knowledge." It was his habit to rest a superstructure on foundations.

The college graduate is far more immature than her characteristic self-reliance leads us to suppose. By her side, the girl who has left school at eighteen, and has lived four years in the world, is weighted with experience. The extension of youth is surely as great a boon to women as to men. There is time enough ahead of all of us in which to grow old and circumspect. For four years the student's interests have been keen and concentrated, the healthy, limited interests of a community. For four years her pleasures have been simple and sane. For four years her ambitions, like the ambitions of her college brother, have been as deeply concerned with athletics as with text-books. She has had a better chance for physical development than if she had "come out" at eighteen. Her college life has been exceptionally happy, because its complications have been few, and its freedom as wide as wisdom would permit. The system of self-government, now introduced into the colleges, has justified itself beyond all questioning. It has promoted a clear understanding of honour, it has taught the student the value of discipline, it has lent dignity to the routine of her life.

> Some reverence for the laws ourselves have made,

is surely the first and best lesson which the citizen of a republic needs to learn.

Writers on educational themes have pointed out — with tremors of apprehension — that while a woman student working among men at a foreign university is mentally stimulated by her surroundings, stimulated often to the point of scholarship, her development is not uniform and normal. She is always in danger of sinking her femininity, or of over-emphasizing it. In the former case, she loses charm and personality; in the latter, sanity and balance. From both perils the college woman in the United States is happily exempt. President Jordan offers as a plea for co-education the healthy sense of companionship between boy and girl students. "There is less of silliness and folly," he says, "where man is not a novelty." But, in truth, this particular form of silliness and folly is at a discount in every woman's college, simply because the interests and occupations which crowd the student's day leave little room for its expansion.

The three best things about the college life of girls are its attitude towards money (an attitude which contrasts sharply with that of many private schools), its attitude towards social disparities, and its attitude towards men. The atmosphere of the college is reasonably democratic. Like gravitates towards like, and a similarity of background and tradition forms a natural basis for companionship; but there is tolerance for other backgrounds which are not without dignity, though they may be lacking in distinction. Poverty is admittedly inconvenient, but carries no reproach. Light hearts and jesting tongues minimize its discomforts. I well remember when the coming of Madame Bernhardt to Philadelphia in 1901 fired the students of Bryn Mawr College with the justifiable ambition to see this great actress in all her finer rôles. Those who had money spent it royally. Those who had none offered their possessions, — books, ornaments, tea-cups, for sale. "Such a chance to buy bargains," observed one young spendthrift, who had been endeavouring to dispose of all she needed most; "but unluckily everybody wants to sell. We know now the importance of the consuming classes, and how useful in their modest way some idle rich would be."

That large and influential portion of the community which does not know its own mind, and which the rest of the world is always endeavouring to conciliate, is still divided between its honest desire to educate women, and its fear lest the woman, when educated, may lose the conservative force which is her most valuable asset. That small and combative portion of the community which knows its own mind accurately, and which always demands the impossible, is determined that the college girl shall betake herself to practical pursuits, that she shall wedge into her four years of work, courses in domestic science, the chemistry of food, nursing, dressmaking, house sanitation, pedagogy, and that blight of the nursery, — child-study. These are the things, we are often told, which it behooves a woman to know, and by the mastery of which she is able, so says a censorious writer in the "Educational Review," "to repay in some measure her debt to man, who has extended to her the benefits of a higher education."

It is to be feared that the girl graduate, the youthful bachelor of arts who steps smiling through the serried ranks of students, her heart beating gladly in response to their generous applause, has little thought of repaying her debt to man. Somebody has made an address which she was too nervous to hear, and has affirmed, with that impressiveness which we all lend to our easiest generalizations, that the purpose of college is to give women a broad and liberal education, and, at the same time, to preserve and develop the characteristics of a complete womanhood. Somebody else has followed up the address with a few fervent remarks, declaring that the only proof of competence is performance. "The world belongs to those who have stormed it." This last ringing sentence — delivered with an almost defiant air of originality — has perhaps caught the graduate's ear, but its familiar cadence awakened no response. Has she not already stormed the world by taking her degree, and does not the world belong to her, in any case, by virtue of her youth and inexperience? Never, while she lives, will it be so completely hers as on the day of her graduation. Let her enjoy her possession while she may.

And her equipment? Well, those of us who call to mind the medley of unstable facts, untenable theories, and undesirable accomplishments, which was *our* substitute for education, deem her solidly informed. If the wisdom of the college president has rescued her from domestic science, and her own common sense has steered her clear of art, she has had a chance, in four years of study, to lay the foundation of knowledge. Her vocabulary is curiously limited. At her age, her grandmother, if a gentlewoman, used more words, and used them better. But then her grandmother had not associated exclusively with youthful companions. The graduate has serious views of life, which are not amiss, and a healthy sense of humour to enliven them. She is resourceful, honourable, and pathetically self-reliant. In her highest and happiest development, she merits the noble words in which an old Ferrara chronicler praises the loveliest and the most maligned woman in all history: "The lady is keen and intellectual, joyous and human, and possesses good reasoning powers."

To balance these permanent gains, there are some temporary losses. The college student, if she does not take up a definite line of work, is apt, for a time at least, to be unquiet. That quality so lovingly described by Peacock as "stay-athomeativeness" is her least noticeable characteristic. The smiling discharge of uncongenial social duties, which disciplines the woman of the world, seems to her unseeing eyes a waste of time and opportunities. She has read little, and that little, not for "human delight." Excellence in literature has been pointed out to her, starred and double-starred, like Baedeker's cathedrals. She has been taught the value of standards, and has been spared the groping of the undirected reader, who builds up her own standards slowly and hesitatingly by an endless process of comparison. The saving in time is beneficial, and some defects in taste have been remedied. But human delight does not respond to authority. It is the hour of rapturous reading and the power of secret thinking which make for personal distinction. The shipwreck of education, says Dr. William James, is to be unable, after years of study, to recognize unticketed eminence. The best result obtainable from college, with its liberal and honourable traditions, is that training in the humanities which lifts the raw boy and girl into the ranks of the understanding; enabling them to sympathize with men's mistakes, to feel the beauty of lost causes, the pathos of misguided epochs, "the ceaseless whisper of permanent ideals."

The Estranging Sea

"God bless the narrow sea which keeps her off,
And keeps our Britain whole within itself."

SO speaks "the Tory member's elder son," in "The Princess":—

". . . God bless the narrow seas!
I wish they were a whole Atlantic broad";

and the transatlantic reader, pausing to digest this conservative sentiment, wonders what difference a thousand leagues would make. If the little strip of roughened water which divides Dover from Calais were twice the ocean's breadth, could the division be any wider and deeper than it is?

We Americans cross from continent to continent, and are merged blissfully into the Old-World life. Inured from infancy to contrasts, we seldom resent the unfamiliar. Our attitude towards it is, for the most part, frankly receptive, and full of joyous possibilities. We take kindly, or at least tolerantly, to foreign creeds and customs. We fail to be affronted by what we do not understand. We are not without a shadowy conviction that there may be other points of view than our own, other beliefs than those we have been taught to cherish. Mr. Birrell, endeavouring to account for Charlotte Brontë's hostility to the Belgians, — who had been uncommonly kind to her, — says that she "had never any patience" with Catholicism. The remark invites the reply of the Papal chamberlain to Prince Herbert Bismarck, when that nobleman, being in attendance upon the Emperor, pushed rudely — and unbidden — into Pope Leo's audience chamber. "I am Prince Herbert Bismarck," shouted the German. "That," said the urbane Italian, "explains, but does not excuse your conduct."

So much has been said and written about England's "splendid isolation," the phrase has grown so familiar to English eyes and ears, that the political and social attitude which it represents is a source of pride to thousands of Englishmen who are intelligent enough to know what isolation costs. "It is of the utmost importance," says the "Spectator," "that we should understand that the temper with which England regards the other states of Europe, and the temper with which those states regard her, is absolutely different." And then, with ill-concealed elation, the writer adds: "The English are the most universally disliked nation on the face of the earth."

Diplomatically, this may be true, though it is hard to see why. Socially and individually, it is not true at all. The English possess too many agreeable traits to permit them to be as much disliked as they think and hope they are. Even on the Continent, even in that strange tourist world where hostilities grow apace, where the courtesies of life are relaxed, and where every nationality presents its least lovable aspect, the English can never aspire to the prize of unpopularity. They are too silent, too clean, too handsome, too fond of fresh air, too schooled in the laws of justice which compel them to acknowledge—however reluctantly—the rights of other men. They are certainly uncivil, but that is a matter of no great moment. We do not demand that our fellow tourists should be urbane, but that they should evince a sense of propriety in their behaviour, that they should be decently reluctant to annoy. There is distinction in the Englishman's quietude, and in his innate respect for order.

But why should he covet alienation? Why should he dread popularity, lest it imply that he resembles other men? When the tide of fortune turned in the South African war, and the news of the relief of Mafeking drove London mad with joy, there were Englishmen who expressed grave alarm at the fervid demonstrations of the populace. England, they said, was wont to take her defeats without despondency, and her victories without elation. They feared the national character was changing, and becoming more like the character of Frenchmen and Americans.

This apprehension — happily unfounded — was very insular and very English. National traits are, as a matter of fact, as enduring as the mountain-tops. They survive all change of policies, all shifting of boundary lines, all expansion and contraction of dominion. When Froissart tranquilly observed, "The English are affable to no other nation than themselves," he spoke for the centuries to come. Sorbières, who visited England in 1663, who loved the English turf, hated and feared the English cooking, and deeply admired his hospitable English hosts, admitted that the nation had "a propensity to scorn all the rest of the world." The famous verdict, "*Les Anglais sont justes, mais pas bons*," crystallizes the judgment of time. Foreign opinion is necessarily an imperfect diagnosis, but it has its value to the open mind. He is a wise man who heeds it, and a dull man who holds it in derision. When an English writer in "Macmillan" remarks with airy contempt that French criticisms on England have "all the piquancy of a woman's criticisms on a man," the American — standing outside the ring — is amused by this superb simplicity of self-conceit.

Fear of a French invasion and the carefully nurtured detestation of the Papacy, — these two controlling influences must be held responsible for prejudices too deep to be fathomed, too strong to be overcome. "We do naturally hate the French," observes Mr. Pepys, with genial candour; and this ordinary, everyday prejudice darkened into fury when Napoleon's conquests menaced the world.

Our school histories have taught us (it is the happy privilege of a school history to teach us many things which make no impression on our minds) that for ten years England apprehended a descent upon her shores; but we cannot realize what the apprehension meant, how it ate its way into the hearts of men, until we stumble upon some such paragraph as this, from a letter of Lord Jeffrey's, written to Francis Horner in the winter of 1808: "For my honest impression is that Bonaparte will be in Dublin in about fifteen months, perhaps. And then, if I survive, I shall try to go to America."

"If I survive!" What wonder that Jeffrey, who was a clear-headed, unimaginative man, cherished all his life a cold hostility to France? What wonder that the painter Haydon, who was highly imaginative and not in the least clear-headed, felt such hostility to be an essential part of patriotism? "In *my* day," he writes in his journal, "boys were born, nursed, and grew up, hating and to hate the name of Frenchman." He did hate it with all his heart, but then his earliest recollection — when he was but four years old — was seeing his mother lying on her sofa and crying bitterly. He crept up to her, puzzled and frightened, poor baby, and she sobbed out: "They have cut off the Queen of France's head, my dear." Such an ineffaceable recollection colours childhood and sets character. It is an education for life.

As for the Papacy, — well, years have softened but not destroyed England's hereditary detestation of Rome. The easy tolerance of the American for any religion, or for all religions, or for no religion at all, is the natural outcome of a mixed nationality, and of a tolerably serene background. We have shed very little of our blood, or of our neighbour's blood, for the faith that was in us, or in him; and, during the past half-century, forbearance has broadened into unconcern. Even the occasional refusal of a pastor to allow a cleric of another denomination to preach in his church, can hardly be deemed a violent form of persecution.

What American author, for example, can recall such childish memories as those which Mr. Edmund Gosse describes with illuminating candour in "Father and Son"? "We welcomed any social disorder in any part of Italy, as likely to be annoying to the Papacy. If there was a custom-house officer stabbed in a fracas at Sassari, we gave loud thanks that liberty and light were breaking in upon Sardinia." What American scientist, taking a holiday in Italy, ever carried around with him such uncomfortable sensations as those described by Professor Huxley in some of his Roman letters? "I must have a strong strain of Puritan blood in me somewhere," he writes to Sir John Donnelly, after a morning spent at Saint Peter's, "for I am possessed with a desire to arise and slay the whole brood of idolaters, whenever I assist at one of these services."

Save and except Miss Georgiana Podsnap's faltering fancy for murdering her partners at a ball, this is the most bloodthirsty sentiment on record, and suggests but a limited enjoyment of a really beautiful service. Better the light-hearted unconcern of Mr. John Richard Green, the historian, who, albeit a clergyman of the Church of England, preferred going to the Church of Rome when Catholicism had an organ, and Protestantism, a harmonium. "The difference in truth between them does n't seem to me to make up for the difference in instruments."

Mr. Lowell speaks somewhere of a "divine provincialism," which expresses the sturdy sense of a nation, and is but ill replaced by a cosmopolitanism lacking in virtue and distinction. Perhaps this is England's gift, and insures for her a solidarity which Americans lack. Ignoring or misunderstanding the standards of other races, she sets her own so high we needs must raise our eyes to consider them. Yet when Mr. Arnold scandalized his fellow countrymen by the frank confession that he found foreign life "liberating," what did he mean but that he refused to

> "drag at each remove a lengthening chain"?

His mind leaped gladly to meet new issues and fresh tides of thought; he stood ready to accept the reasonableness of usages which differed materially from his own; and he took delight in the trivial happenings of every day, precisely because they were un-English and unfamiliar. Even the names of strange places, of German castles and French villages, gave him, as they give Mr. Henry James, a curious satisfaction, a sense of harmony and ordered charm.

In that caustic volume, "Elizabeth in Rügen," there is an amusing description of the indignation of the bishop's wife,

Mrs. Harvey-Browne, over what she considers the stupidities of German speech.

"What," she asks with asperity, "could be more supremely senseless than calling the Baltic the Ostsee?"

"Well, but why should n't they, if they want to?" says Elizabeth densely.

"But, dear Frau X, it is so foolish. East sea! Of what is it the east? One is always the east of something, but one does n't talk about it. The name has no meaning whatever. Now 'Baltic' exactly describes it."

This is fiction, but it is fiction easily surpassed by fact, — witness the English tourist in France who said to Sir Leslie Stephen that it was "unnatural" for soldiers to dress in blue. Then, remembering certain British instances, he added hastily: "Except, indeed, for the Artillery, or the Blue Horse." "The English model," comments Sir Leslie, "with all its variations, appeared to him to be ordained by nature."

The rigid application of one nation's formulas to another nation's manners has its obvious disadvantages. It is praiseworthy in an Englishman to carry his conscience — like his bathtub — wherever he goes, but both articles are sadly in his way. The American who leaves his conscience and his tub at home, and who trusts to being clean and good after a foreign fashion, has an easier time, and is not permanently stained. Being less cock-sure in the start about his standing with Heaven, he is subject to reasonable doubts as to the culpability of other people. The joyous outdoor Sundays of France and Germany please him at least as well as the shut-in Sundays of England and Scotland. He takes kindly to concerts, enlivened, without demoralization, by beer, and wonders why he cannot have them at home. Whatever is distinctive, whatever is national, interests and delights him; and he seldom feels called upon to decide a moral issue which is not submitted to his judgment.

I was once in Valais when a rude play was acted by the peasants of Vissoye. It set forth the conversion of the Huns to Christianity through the medium of a miracle vouchsafed to Zachéo, the legendary apostle of Anniviers. The little stage was erected on a pleasant hillside, the procession bearing the cross wound down from the village church, the priests from all the neighbouring towns were present, and the pious Valaisans — as overjoyed as if the Huns were a matter of yesterday — sang a solemn *Te Deum* in thanksgiving for the conversion of their land. It would be hard to conceive of a drama less profane; indeed, only religious fervour could have breathed life into so much controversy; yet I had English friends, intelligent, cultivated, and deeply interested, who refused to go with me to Vissoye because it was Sunday afternoon. They stood by their guns, and attended their own service in the drawing-room of the deserted little hotel at Zinal; gaining, I trust, the approval of their own consciences, and losing the experience of a lifetime.

Disapprobation has ever been a powerful stimulus to the Saxon mind. The heroic measures which it enforces command our faltering homage, and might incite us to emulation, were we not temperamentally disposed to ask ourselves the fatal question, "Is it worth while?" When we remember that twenty-five thousand people in Great Britain left off eating sugar, by way of protest against slavery in the West Indies, we realize how the individual Englishman holds himself morally responsible for wrongs he is innocent of inflicting, and powerless to redress. Hood and other light-minded humourists laughed at him for drinking bitter tea; but he was not to be shaken by ridicule. Miss Edgeworth voiced the conservative sentiment of her day when she objected to eating unsweetened custards; but he was not to be chilled by apathy.

The same strenuous spirit impelled the English to express their sympathy for Captain Alfred Dreyfus by staying away from the Paris fair of 1900. The London press loudly boasted that Englishmen would not give the sanction of their presence to any undertaking of the French Government, and called attention again and again to their absence from the exhibition. I myself was asked a number of times in England whether this absence were a noticeable thing; but truth compelled me to admit that it was not. With Paris brimming over like a cup filled to the lip, with streets and fair-grounds thronged, with every hotel crowded and every cab engaged, and with twenty thousand of my own countrymen clamorously enlivening the scene, it was not possible to miss anybody anywhere.

It obviously had not occurred to Americans to see any connection between the trial of Captain Dreyfus and their enjoyment of the most beautiful and brilliant thing that Europe had to give. The pretty adage, "*Tout homme a deux pays : le sien et puis la France*," is truer of us than of any other people in the world. And we may as well pardon a nation her transgressions, if we cannot keep away from her shores.

England's public utterances anent the United States are of the friendliest character. Her newspapers and magazines say flattering things about us. Her poet-laureate — unlike his great predecessor who unaffectedly detested us — began his official career by praising us with such fervour that we felt we ought in common honesty to tell him that we were nothing like so good as he thought us. An English text-book, published a few years ago, explains generously to the school-boys of Great Britain that the

United States should not be looked upon as a foreign nation. "They are peopled by men of our blood and faith, enjoy in a great measure the same laws that we do, read the same Bible, and acknowledge, like us, the rule of King Shakespeare."

All this is very pleasant, but the fact remains that Englishmen express surprise and pain at our most innocent idiosyncrasies. They correct our pronunciation and our misuse of words. They regret our nomadic habits, our shrill voices, our troublesome children, our inability to climb mountains or "do a little glacier work" (it sounds like embroidery, but means scrambling perilously over ice), our taste for unwholesome — or, in other words, seasoned — food. When I am reproved by English acquaintances for the "Americanisms" which disfigure my speech and proclaim my nationality, I cannot well defend myself by asserting that I read the same Bible as they do, — for maybe, after all, I don't.

The Estranging Sea

The tenacity with which English residents on the Continent cling to the customs and traditions of their own country is pathetic in its loyalty and in its misconceptions. Their scheme of life does not permit a single foreign observance, their range of sympathies seldom includes a single foreign ideal. "An Englishman's happiness," says M. Taine, "consists in being at home at six in the evening, with a pleasing, attached wife, four or five children, and respectful domestics." This is a very good notion of happiness, no fault can be found with it, and something on the same order, though less perfect in detail, is highly prized and commended in America. But it does not embrace every avenue of delight. The Frenchman who seems never to go home, who seldom has a large family, whose wife is often his business partner and helpmate, and whose servants are friendly allies rather than automatic menials, enjoys life also, and with some degree of intelligence. He may be pardoned for resenting the attitude of English exiles, who, driven from their own country by the harshness of the climate, or the cruel cost of living, never cease to deplore the unaccountable foreignness of foreigners. "Our social tariff amounts to prohibition," said a witty Englishman in France. "Exchange of ideas takes place only at the extreme point of necessity."

It is not under such conditions that any nation gives its best to strangers. It is not to the affronted soul that the charm of the unfamiliar makes its sweet and powerful appeal. Lord Byron was furious when one of his countrywomen called Chamonix "rural"; yet, after all, the poor creature was giving the scenery what praise she understood. The Englishman who complained that he could not look out of his window in Rome without seeing the sun, had a legitimate grievance (we all know what it is to sigh for grey skies, and for the unutterable rest they bring); but if we want Rome, we must take her sunshine, along with her beggars and her Church. Accepted sympathetically, they need not mar our infinite content.

There is a wonderful sentence in Mrs. Humphry Ward's "Marriage of William Ashe," which subtly and strongly protests against the blight of mental isolation. Lady Kitty Bristol is reciting Corneille in Lady Grosville's drawing-room. "Her audience," says Mrs. Ward, "looked on at first with the embarrassed or hostile air which is the Englishman's natural protection against the great things of art." To write a sentence at once so caustic and so flawless is to triumph over the limitations of language. The reproach seems a strange one to hurl at a nation which has produced the noblest literature of the world since the light of Greece waned; but we must remember that distinction of mind, as Mrs. Ward understands it, and as it was understood by Mr. Arnold, is necessarily allied with a knowledge of French arts and letters, and with some insight into the qualities which clarify French conversation. "Divine provincialism" had no halo for the man who wrote "Friendship's Garland." He regarded it with an impatience akin to mistrust, and bordering upon fear. Perhaps the final word was spoken long ago by a writer whose place in literature is so high that few aspire to read him. England was severing her sympathies sharply from much which she had held in common with the rest of Europe, when Dryden wrote: "They who would combat general authority with particular opinion must first establish themselves a reputation of understanding better than other men."

Travellers' Tales

"Wenten forth in heore wey with mony wyse tales,
And hedden leve to lyen al heore lyf aftir."
Piers Plowman.

I DON'T know about travellers' "hedden leve" to lie, but that they "taken leve" no one can doubt who has ever followed their wandering footsteps. They say the most charming and audacious things, in blessed indifference to the fact that somebody may possibly believe them. They start strange hopes and longings in the human heart, and they pave the way for disappointments and disasters. They record the impression of a careless hour as though it were the experience of a lifetime.

There is a delightful little book on French rivers, written some years ago by a vivacious and highly imaginative gentleman named Molloy. It is a rose-tinted volume from the first page to the last, so full of gay adventures that it would lure a mollusc from his shell. Every town and every village yields some fresh delight, some humorous exploit to the four oarsmen who risk their lives to see it; but the few pages devoted to Amboise are of a dulcet and irresistible persuasiveness. They fill the reader's soul with a haunting desire to lay down his well-worn cares and pleasures, to say good-bye to home and kindred, and to seek that favoured spot. Touraine is full of beauty, and steeped to the lips in historic crimes. Turn where we may, her fairness charms the eye, her memories stir the heart. But Mr. Molloy claims for Amboise something rarer in France than loveliness or romance, something which no French town has ever yet been known to possess, — a slumberous and soul-satisfying silence. "We dropped under the very walls of the Castle," he writes, "without seeing a soul. It was a strange contrast to Blois in its absolute stillness. There was no sound but the noise of waters rushing through the arches of the bridge. It might have been the palace of the Sleeping Beauty, but was only one of the retrospective cities that had no concern with the present."

Quiet brooded over the ivied towers and ancient water front. Tranquillity, unconcern, a gentle and courteous aloofness surrounded and soothed the intrepid travellers. When, in the early morning, the crew pushed off in their frail boat, less than a dozen citizens assembled to watch the start. Even the peril of the performance (and there are few things more likely to draw a crowd than the chance of seeing four fellow mortals drown) failed to awaken curiosity. Nine men stood silent on the shore when the outrigger shot into the swirling river, and it is the opinion of the chronicler that Amboise "did not often witness such a gathering." Nine quiet men were, for Amboise, something in the nature of a mob.

It must be remembered that Mr. Molloy's book is not a new one; but then Touraine is neither new nor mutable. Nothing changes in its beautiful old towns, the page of whose history has been turned for centuries. What if motors now whirl in a white dust through the heart of France? They do not affect the lives of the villages through which they pass. The simple and primitive desire of the motorist is to be fed and to move on, to be fed again and to move on again, to sleep and to start afresh. That unavoidable waiting between trains which now and then compelled an old-time tourist to look at a cathedral or a château, by way of diverting an empty hour, no longer retards progress. The motorist needs never wait. As soon as he has eaten, he can go, — a privilege of which he gladly avails himself. A month at

Amboise taught us that, at the feeding-hour, motors came flocking like fowls, and then, like fowls, dispersed. They were disagreeable while they lasted, but they never lasted long. Replete with a five-course luncheon, their fagged and grimy occupants sped on to distant towns and dinner.

But why should we, who knew well that there is not, and never has been, a quiet corner in all France, have listened to a traveller's tale, and believed in a silent Amboise? Is there no limit to human credulity? Does experience count for nothing in the Bourbon-like policy of our lives? It is to England we must go if we seek for silence, that gentle, pervasive silence which wraps us in a mantle of content. It was in Porlock that Coleridge wrote "Kubla Khan," transported, Heaven knows whither, by virtue of the hushed repose that consecrates the sleepiest hamlet in Great Britain. It was at Stoke Pogis that Gray composed his "Elegy." He could never have written—

> "And all the air a solemn stillness holds,"

in the vicinity of a French village.

But Amboise! Who would go to rural England, live on ham and eggs, and sleep in a bed harder than Pharaoh's heart, if it were possible that a silent Amboise awaited him? The fair fresh vegetables of France, her ripe red strawberries and glowing cherries, her crisp salads and her caressing mattresses lured us no less than the vision of a blood-stained castle, and the wide sweep of the Loire flashing through the joyous landscape of Touraine. In the matter of beauty, Amboise outstrips all praise. In the matter of romance, she leaves nothing to be desired. Her splendid old Château—half palace and half fortress—towers over the river which mirrors its glory and perpetuates its shame. She is a storehouse of historic memories, she is the loveliest of little towns, she is in the heart of a district which bears the finest fruit and has the best cooks in France; but she is not, and never has been, silent, since the days when Louis the Eleventh was crowned, and she gave wine freely to all who chose to be drunk and merry at her charge.

If she does not give her wine to-day, she sells it so cheaply — lying girt by vine-clad hills — that many of her sons are drunk and merry still. The sociable habit of setting a table in the open street prevails at Amboise. Around it labourers take their evening meal, to the accompaniment of song and sunburnt mirth. It sounds poetic and it looks picturesque, — like a picture by Teniers or Jan Steen, — but it is not a habit conducive to repose.

As far as I can judge, — after a month's experience, — the one thing no inhabitant of Amboise ever does is to go to bed. At midnight the river front is alive with cheerful and strident voices. The French countryman habitually speaks to his neighbour as if he were half a mile away; and when a score of countrymen are conversing in this key, the air rings with their clamour. They sing in the same lusty fashion; not through closed lips, as is the custom of English singers, but rolling out the notes with volcanic energy from the deep craters of their throats. When our admirable waiter—who is also our best friend—frees his soul in song as he is setting the table, the walls of the dining-room quiver and vibrate. By five o'clock in the morning every one except ourselves is on foot and out of doors. We might as well be, for it is custom, not sleep, which keeps us in our beds. The hay wagons are rolling over the bridge, the farmhands are going to work, the waiter, in an easy undress, is exchanging voluble greetings with his many acquaintances, the life of the town has begun.

The ordinary week-day life, I mean, for on Sundays the market people have assembled by four, and there are nights when the noises never cease. It is no unusual thing to be awakened, an hour or two after midnight, by a tumult so loud and deep that my first impression is one of conspiracy or revolution. The sound is not unlike the hoarse roar of Sir Henry Irving's admirably trained mobs, — the only mobs I have ever heard, — and I jump out of bed, wondering if the President has been shot, or the Chamber of Deputies blown up by malcontents. Can these country people have heard the news, as the shepherds of Peloponnesus heard of the fall of Syracuse, through the gossiping of wood devils, and, like the shepherds, have hastened to carry the intelligence? When I look out of my window, the crowd seems small for the uproar it is making. Armand, the waiter, who, I am convinced, merely dozes on a dining-room chair, so as to be in readiness for any diversion, stands in the middle of the road, gesticulating with fine dramatic gestures. I cannot hear what is being said, because everybody is speaking at once; but after a while the excitement dies away, and the group slowly disperses, shouting final vociferations from out of the surrounding darkness. The next day when I ask the cause of the disturbance, Armand looks puzzled at my question. He does not seem aware that anything out of the way has happened; but finally explains that "quelques amis" were passing the hotel, and that Madame must have heard them stop and talk. The incident is apparently too common an occurrence to linger in his mind.

As for the Amboise dogs, I do not know whether they really possess a supernatural strength which enables them to bark twenty-four hours without intermission, or whether they divide themselves into day and night pickets, so that, when one band retires to rest, the other takes up the interrupted duty. The French villager, who values all domestic pets in proportion to the noise they can make, delights especially in his dogs, giant black-and-tan terriers for the most part, of indefatigable perseverance in their one line of activity. Their bark is high-pitched and querulous rather than deep and defiant, but for continuity it has no rival upon earth. Our hotel — in all other respects unexceptionable — possesses two large bulldogs which have long ago lost their British phlegm, and acquired the agitated yelp of their Gallic neighbours. They could not be quiet if they wanted to, for heavy sleigh-bells (unique decorations for a bulldog) hang about their necks, and jangle merrily at every step. In the courtyard lives a colony of birds. One virulent parrot which shrieks its inarticulate wrath from morning until night, but which does — be it remembered to its credit — go to sleep at sundown; three paroquets; two cockatoos of ineffable shrillness, and a cageful of canaries and captive finches. When taken in connection with the dogs, the hotel cat, the operatic Armand, and the cook who plays "See, O Norma!" on his flute every afternoon and evening, it will be seen that Amboise does not so closely resemble the palace of the Sleeping Beauty as Mr. Molloy has given us to understand.

All other sounds, however, melt into a harmonious murmur when compared to the one great speciality of the village, — stone-cutting in the open streets. Whenever one of the picturesque old houses is crumbling into utter decay, a pile of stone is dumped before it, and the easy-going masons of Amboise prepare to patch up its walls. No particular method is observed, the work progresses after the fashion of a child's block house, and the principal labour lies in dividing the lumps of stone. This is done with a rusty old saw pulled slowly backward and forward by two men, the sound produced resembling a succession of agonized shrieks. It goes on for hours and hours, with no apparent result except the noise; while a handsome boy, in a striped blouse and broad blue sash, completes the discord by currying the stone with an iron currycomb,—a process I have never witnessed before, and ardently hope never to witness again. If one could imagine fifty school-children all squeaking their slate pencils down their slates together,—who does not remember that blood-curdling music of his youth?—one might gain some feeble notion of the acute agony induced by such an instrument of torture. Agony to the nervous visitor alone; for the inhabitants of Amboise love their shrieking saws and currycombs, just as they love their shrieking parrots and cockatoos. They gather in happy crowds to watch the blue-sashed boy, and drink in the noise he makes. We drink it in, too, as he is immediately beneath our windows. Then we look at the castle walls glowing in the splendour of the sunset, and at the Loire sweeping in magnificent curves between the grey-green poplar trees ; at the noble width of the horizon, and at the deepening tints of the sky ; and we realize that a silent Amboise would be an earthly Paradise, too fair for this sinful world.

The Chill of Enthusiasm

"Surtout, pas de zèle." —TALLEYRAND.

THERE is no aloofness so forlorn as our aloofness from an uncontagious enthusiasm, and there is no hostility so sharp as that aroused by a fervour which fails of response. Charles Lamb's "D—n him at a hazard," was the expression of a natural and reasonable frame of mind with which we are all familiar, and which, though admittedly unlovely, is in the nature of a safeguard. If we had no spiritual asbestos to protect our souls, we should be consumed to no purpose by every wanton flame. If our sincere and restful indifference to things which concern us not were shaken by every blast, we should have no available force for things which concern us deeply. If eloquence did not sometimes make us yawn, we should be besotted by oratory. And if we did not approach new acquaintances, new authors, and new points of view with life-saving reluctance, we should never feel that vital regard which, being strong enough to break down our barriers, is strong enough to hold us for life.

The worth of admiration is, after all, in proportion to the value of the thing admired,—a circumstance overlooked by the people who talk much pleasant nonsense about sympathy, and the courage of our emotions, and the open and generous mind. We know how Mr. Arnold felt when an American lady wrote to him, in praise of American authors, and said that it rejoiced her heart to think of such excellence as being "common and abundant." Mr. Arnold, who considered that excellence of any kind was very uncommon and beyond measure rare, expressed his views on this occasion with more fervour and publicity than the circumstances demanded; but his words are as balm to the irritation which some of us suffer and conceal when drained of our reluctant applause.

It is perhaps because women have been trained to a receptive attitude of mind, because for centuries they have been valued for their sympathy and appreciation rather than for their judgment, that they are so perilously prone to enthusiasm. It has come to all of us of late to hear much feminine eloquence, and to marvel at the nimbleness of woman's wit, at the speed with which she thinks, and the facility with which she expresses her thoughts. A woman who, until five years ago, never addressed a larger audience than that afforded by a reading-club or a dinner-party, will now thrust and parry on a platform, wholly unembarrassed by timidity or by ignorance. Sentiment and satire are hers to command; and while neither is convincing, both are tremendously effective with people already convinced, with the partisans who throng unwearyingly to hear the voicing of their own opinions. The ease with which such a speaker brings forward the great central fact of the universe, maternity, as an argument for or against the casting of a ballot (it works just as well either way); the glow with which she associates Jeanne d'Arc with federated clubs and social service; and the gay defiance she hurls at customs and prejudices so profoundly obsolete that the lantern of Diogenes could not find them lurking in a village street, — these things may chill the unemotional listener into apathy, but they never fail to awaken the sensibilities of an audience. The simple process, so highly commended by debaters, of ignoring all that cannot be denied, makes demonstration easy. "A crowd," said Mr. Ruskin, "thinks by infection." To be immune from infection is to stand outside the sacred circle of enthusiasts.

Yet if the experience of mankind teaches anything, it is that vital convictions are not at the mercy of eloquence. The "oratory of conviction," to borrow a phrase of Mr. Bagehot's, is so rare as to be hardly worth taking into account. Fox used to say that if a speech read well, it was "a damned bad speech," which is the final word of cynicism, spoken by one who knew. It was the saving sense of England, that solid, prosaic, dependable common sense, the bulwark of every great nation, which, after Sheridan's famous speech, demanding the impeachment of Warren Hastings, made the House adjourn "to collect its reason,"—obviously because its reason had been lost. Sir William Dolden, who moved the adjournment, frankly confessed that it was impossible to give a "determinate opinion" while under the spell of oratory. So the lawmakers, who had been fired to white heat, retired to cool down again; and when Sheridan—always as deep in difficulties as Micawber—was offered a thousand pounds for the manuscript of the speech, he remembered Fox's verdict, and refused to risk his unballasted eloquence in print.

Enthusiasm is praised because it implies an unselfish concern for something outside our personal interest and advancement. It is reverenced because the great and wise amendments, which from time to time straighten the roads we walk, may always be traced back to somebody's zeal for reform. It is rich in prophetic attributes, banking largely on the unknown, and making up in nobility of design what it lacks in excellence of attainment. Like simplicity, and candour, and other much-commended qualities, enthusiasm is charming until we meet it face to face, and cannot escape from its charm. It is then that we begin to understand the attitude of Goethe, and Talleyrand,

and Pitt, and Sir Robert Peel, who saved themselves from being consumed by resolutely refusing to ignite. "It is folly," observed Goethe, "to expect that other men will consent to believe as we do"; and, having reconciled himself to this elemental obstinacy of the human heart, it no longer troubled him that those whom he felt to be wrong should refuse to acknowledge their errors.

There are men and women — not many — who have the happy art of making their most fervent convictions endurable. Their hobbies do not spread desolation over the social world, their prejudices do not insult our intelligence. They may be so "abreast with the times" that we cannot keep track of them, or they may be basking serenely in some Early Victorian close. They may believe buoyantly in the Baconian cipher, or in thought transference, or in the serious purposes of Mr. George Bernard Shaw, or in anything else which invites credulity. They may even express their views, and still be loved and cherished by their friends.

How illuminating is the contrast which Hazlitt unconsciously draws between the enthusiasms of Lamb which everybody was able to bear, and the enthusiasms of Coleridge which nobody was able to bear. Lamb would parade his admiration for some favourite author, Donne, for example, whom the rest of the company probably abhorred. He would select the most crabbed passages to quote and defend; he would stammer out his piquant and masterful half sentences, his scalding jests, his controvertible assertions; he would skilfully hint at the defects which no one else was permitted to see; and if he made no converts (wanting none), he woke no weary wrath. But we all have a sneaking sympathy for Holcroft, who, when Coleridge was expatiating rapturously and oppressively upon the glories of German transcendental philosophy, and upon his own supreme command of the field, cried out suddenly and with exceeding bitterness: "Mr. Coleridge, you are the most eloquent man I ever met, and the most unbearable in your eloquence."

I am not without a lurking suspicion that George Borrow must have been at times unbearable in his eloquence. "We cannot refuse to meet a man on the ground that he is an enthusiast," observes Mr. George Street, obviously lamenting this circumstance; "but we should at least like to make sure that his enthusiasms are under control." Borrow's enthusiasms were never under control. He stood ready at a moment's notice to prove the superiority of the Welsh bards over the paltry poets of England, or to relate the marvellous Welsh prophecies, so vague as to be always safe. He was capable of inflicting Armenian verbs upon Isopel Berners when they sat at night over their gipsy kettle in the dingle (let us hope she fell asleep as sweetly as does Milton's Eve when Adam grows too garrulous); and he met the complaints of a poor farmer on the hardness of the times with jubilant praises of evangelicalism. "Better pay three pounds an acre, and live on crusts and water in the present enlightened days," he told the disheartened husbandman, "than pay two shillings an acre, and sit down to beef and ale three times a day in the old superstitious ages." This is *not* the oratory of conviction. There are unreasoning prejudices in favour of one's own stomach which eloquence cannot gainsay. "I defy the utmost power of language to disgust me wi' a gude denner," observes the Ettrick Shepherd; thus putting on record the attitude of the bucolic mind, impassive, immutable, since earth's first harvests were gleaned.

The artificial emotions which expand under provocation, and collapse when the provocation is withdrawn, must be held responsible for much mental confusion.

The Chill of Enthusiasm

Election oratory is an old and cherished institution. It is designed to make candidates show their paces, and to give innocent amusement to the crowd. Properly reinforced by brass bands and bunting, graced by some sufficiently august presence, and enlivened by plenty of cheering and hat-flourishing, it presents a strong appeal. A political party is, moreover, a solid and self-sustaining affair. All sound and alliterative generalities about virile and vigorous manhood, honest and honourable labour, great and glorious causes, are understood, in this country at least, to refer to the virile and vigorous manhood of Republicans or Democrats, as the case may be; and to uphold the honest and honourable, great and glorious Republican or Democratic principles, upon which, it is also understood, depends the welfare of the nation.

Yet even this sense of security cannot always save us from the chill of collapsed enthusiasm. I was once at a great mass meeting, held in the interests of municipal reform, and at which the principal speaker was a candidate for office. He was delayed for a full hour after the meeting had been opened, and this hour was filled with good platform oratory. Speechmaker after speechmaker, all adepts in their art, laid bare before our eyes the evils which consumed us, and called upon us passionately to support the candidate who would lift us from our shame. The fervour of the house rose higher and higher. Martial music stirred our blood, and made us feel that reform and patriotism were one. The atmosphere grew tense with expectancy, when suddenly there came a great shout, and the sound of cheering from the crowd in the streets, the crowd which could not force its way into the huge and closely packed opera house. Now there are few things more profoundly affecting than cheers heard from a distance, or muffled by intervening walls. They have a fine dramatic quality, unknown to the cheers which rend the air about us. When the chairman of the meeting announced that the candidate was outside the doors, speaking to the mob, the excitement reached fever heat. When some one cried, "He is here!" and the orchestra struck the first bars of "Hail Columbia," we rose to our feet, waving multitudinous flags, and shouting out the rapture of our hearts.

And then, — and then there stepped upon the stage a plain, tired, bewildered man, betraying nervous exhaustion in every line. He spoke, and his voice was not the assured voice of a leader. His words were not the happy words which instantly command attention. It was evident to the discerning eye that he had been driven for days, perhaps for weeks, beyond his strength and endurance; that he had resorted to stimulants to help him in this emergency, and that they had failed; that he was striving with feeble desperation to do the impossible which was expected of him. I wondered even then if a few common words of explanation, a few sober words of promise, would not have satisfied the crowd, already sated with eloquence. I wondered if the unfortunate man could feel the chill settling down upon the house as he spoke his random and undignified sentences, whether he could see the first stragglers slipping down the aisles. What did his decent record, his honest purpose, avail him in an hour like this? He tried to lash himself to vigour, but it was spurring a broken-winded horse. The stragglers increased into a flying squadron, the house was emptying fast, when the chairman in sheer desperation made a sign to the leader of the orchestra, who waved his baton, and "The Star-Spangled Banner" drowned the candidate's last words, and brought what was left of the audience to its feet. I turned to a friend beside me, the wife of a local politician who had been the most fiery speaker of the evening. "Will it make any difference?" I asked, and she answered disconsolately; "The city is lost, but we may save the state."

Then we went out into the quiet streets, and I bethought me of Voltaire's driving in a blue coach powdered with gilt stars to see the first production of "Irène," and of his leaving the theatre to find that enthusiasts had cut the traces of his horses, so that the shouting mob might drag him home in triumph. But the mob, having done its shouting, melted away after the irresponsible fashion of mobs, leaving the blue coach stranded in front of the Tuileries, with Voltaire shivering inside of it, until the horses could be brought back, the traces patched up, and the driver recalled to his duty.

That "popular enthusiasm is but a fire of straw" has been amply demonstrated by all who have tried to keep it going. It can be lighted to some purpose, as when money is extracted from the enthusiasts before they have had time to cool; but even this process — so skilfully conducted by the initiated — seems unworthy of great and noble charities, or of great and noble causes. It is true also that the agitator — no matter what he may be agitating — is always sure of his market; a circumstance which made that most conservative of chancellors, Lord Eldon, swear with bitter oaths that, if he were to begin life over again, he would begin it as an agitator. Tom Moore tells a pleasant story (one of the many pleasant stories embalmed in his vast sarcophagus of a diary) about a street orator whom he heard address a crowd in Dublin. The man's eloquence was so stirring that Moore was ravished by it, and he expressed to Sheil his admiration for the speaker. "Ah," said Sheil carelessly, "that was a brewer's patriot. Most of the great brewers have in their employ a regular patriot who goes about among the publicans, talking violent politics, which helps to sell the beer."

Honest enthusiasm, we are often told, is the power which moves the world. Therefore it is perhaps that honest enthusiasts seem to think that if they stopped pushing, the world would stop moving,—as though it were a new world which did n't know its way. This belief inclines them to intolerance. The more keen they are, the more contemptuous they become. What Wordsworth admirably called "the self-applauding sincerity of a heated mind" leaves them no loophole for doubt, and no understanding of the doubter. In their volcanic progress they bowl over the non-partisan—a man and a brother—with splendid unconcern. He, poor soul, stunned but not convinced, clings desperately to some pettifogging convictions which he calls truth, and refuses a clearer vision. His habit of remembering what he believed yesterday clogs his mind, and makes it hard for him to believe something entirely new to-day. Much has been said about the inconvenience of keeping opinions, but much might be said about the serenity of the process. Old opinions are like old friends, — we cease to question their worth because, after years of intimacy and the loss of some valuable illusions, we have grown to place our slow reliance on them. We know at least where we stand, and whither we are tending, and we refuse to bustle feverishly about the circumference of life, because, as Amiel warns us, we cannot reach its core.

The Temptation of Eve

"My Love in her attire doth shew her wit."

IT is an old and honoured jest that Eve — type of eternal womanhood — sacrified the peace of Eden for the pleasures of dress. We see this jest reflected in the satire of the Middle Ages, in the bitter gibes of mummer and buffoon. We can hear its echoes in the invectives of the reformer, — "I doubt," said a good fifteenth-century bishop to the ladies of England in their horned caps, — "I doubt the Devil sit not between those horns." We find it illustrated with admirable naïveté in the tapestries which hang in the entrance corridor of the Belle Arti in Florence.

These tapestries tell the downfall of our first parents. In one we see the newly created and lovely Eve standing by the side of the sleeping Adam, and regarding him with pleasurable anticipation. Another shows us the animals marching in line to be inspected and named. The snail heads the procession and sets the pace. The lion and the tiger stroll gossiping together. The unicorn walks alone, very stiff and proud. Two rats and two mice are closely followed by two sleek cats, who keep them well covered, and plainly await the time when Eve's amiable indiscretion shall assign them their natural prey. In the third tapestry the deed has been done, the apple had been eaten. The beasts are ravening in the background. Adam, already clad, is engaged in fastening a picturesque girdle of leaves around the unrepentant Eve, — for all the world like a modern husband fastening his wife's gown, — while she for the first time gathers up her long fair hair. Her attitude is full of innocent yet indescribable coquetry. The passion for self-adornment had already taken possession of her soul.

Before her lies a future of many cares and some compensations. She is going to work and she is going to weep, but she is also going to dress. The price was hers to pay.

In the hearts of Eve's daughters lies an unspoken convincement that the price was not too dear. As far as feminity is known, or can ever be known, one dominant impulse has never wavered or weakened. In every period of the world's history, in every quarter of the globe, in every stage of savagery or civilization, this elementary instinct has held, and still holds good. The history of the world is largely the history of dress. It is the most illuminating of records, and tells its tale with a candour and completeness which no chronicle can surpass. We all agree in saying that people who reached a high stage of artistic development, like the Greeks and the Italians of the Renaissance, expressed this sense of perfection in their attire; but what we do not acknowledge so frankly is that these same nations encouraged the beauty of dress, even at a ruthless cost, because they felt that in doing so they coöperated with a great natural law,—the law which makes the "wanton lapwing" get himself another crest. They played into nature's hands.

The nations which sought to bully nature, like the Spartans and the Spaniards, passed the severest sumptuary laws; and for proving the power of fundamental forces over the unprofitable wisdom of reformers, there is nothing like a sumptuary law. In 1563 Spanish women of good repute were forbidden to wear jewels or embroideries, — the result being that many preferred to be thought reputationless, rather than abandon their finery. Some years later it was ordained that only women of loose life should be permitted to bare their shoulders; and all dressmakers who furnished the interdicted gowns to others than courtesans were condemned to four years' penal servitude. These were stern measures, — "root and branch" was ever the Spaniard's cry; but he found it easier to stamp out heresy than to eradicate from a woman's heart something which is called vanity, but which is, in truth, an overmastering impulse which she is too wise to endeavour to resist.

As a matter of fact it was a sumptuary law which incited the women of Rome to make their first great public demonstration, and to besiege the Forum as belligerently as the women of England have, in late years, besieged Parliament. The Senate had thought fit to save money for the second Punic War by curtailing all extravagance in dress; and, when the war was over, showed no disposition to repeal a statute which — to the simple masculine mind — seemed productive of nothing but good. Therefore the women gathered in the streets of Rome, demanding the restitution of their ornaments, and deeply scandalizing poor Cato, who could hardly wedge his way through the crowd. His views on this occasion were expressed with the bewildered bitterness of a modern British conservative. He sighed for the good old days when women were under the strict control of their fathers and husbands, and he very plainly told the Senators that if they had maintained their proper authority at home, their wives and daughters would not then be misbehaving themselves in public. "It was not without painful emotions of shame," said this outraged Roman gentleman, "that I just now made my way to the Forum through a herd of women. Our ancestors thought it improper that women should transact any private business without a director. We, it seems, suffer them to interfere in the management of state affairs, and to intrude into the general assemblies. Had I not been restrained by the modesty and dignity of some among them, had I not been unwilling that they should be rebuked by a Consul, I should have said to them: 'What sort of practice is this of running into the streets, and addressing other women's husbands? Could you not have petitioned at home? Are your blandishments more seductive in public than in private, and with other husbands than your own?'"

How natural it all sounds, how modern, how familiar! And with what knowledge of the immutable laws of nature, as opposed to the capricious laws of man, did Lucius Valerius defend the rebellious women of Rome! "Elegance of apparel," he pleaded before the Senate, "and jewels, and ornaments, — these are a woman's badges of distinction; in these she glories and delights; these our ancestors called the woman's world. What else does she lay aside in mourning save her purple and gold? What else does she resume when the mourning is over? How does she manifest her sympathy on occasions of public rejoicing, but by adding to the splendour of her dress?"[1]

Of course the statute was repealed. The only sumptuary laws which defied resistance were those which draped the Venetian gondolas and the Milanese priests in black, and with such restrictions women had no concern.

The symbolism of dress is a subject which has never received its due share of attention, yet it stands for attributes in the human race which otherwise defy analysis. It is interwoven with all our carnal and with all our spiritual instincts. It represents a cunning triumph over hard conditions, a turning of needs into victories. It voices desires and dignities without number, it subjects the importance of the thing done to the importance of the manner of doing it. "Man wears a special dress to kill, to govern, to judge, to preach, to mourn, to play. In every age the fashion in which he retains or

[1] Livy.

discards some portion of this dress denotes a subtle change in his feelings." All visible things are emblematic of invisible forces. Man fixed the association of colours with grief and gladness, he made ornaments the insignia of office, he ordained that fabric should grace the majesty of power.

Yet though we know this well, it is our careless custom to talk about dress, and to write about dress, as if it had no meaning at all; as if the breaking waves of fashion which carry with them the record of pride and gentleness, of distinction and folly, of the rising and shattering of ideals, — "the cut which betokens intellect and talent, the colour which betokens temper and heart," — were guided by no other law than chance, were a mere purposeless tyranny. Historians dwell upon the mad excesses of ruff and farthingale, of pointed shoe and swelling skirt, as if these things stood for nothing in a society forever alternating between rigid formalism and the irrepressible spirit of democracy.

Is it possible to look at a single costume painted by Velasquez without realizing that the Spanish court under Philip the Fourth had lost the mobility which has characterized it in the days of Ferdinand and Isabella, and had hardened into a formalism, replete with dignity, but lacking intelligence, and out of touch with the great social issues of the day? French chroniclers have written page after page of description — aimless and tiresome description, for the most part — of those amazing head-dresses which, at the court of Marie Antoinette, rose to such heights that the ladies looked as if their heads were in the middle of their bodies. They stood seven feet high when their hair was dressed, and a trifle over five when it was n't. The Duchesse de Lauzun wore upon one memorable occasion a head-dress presenting a landscape in high relief on the shore of a stormy lake, ducks swimming on the lake, a sportsman shooting at the ducks, a mill which rose from the crown of her head, a miller's wife courted by an abbé, and a miller placidly driving his donkey down the steep incline over the lady's left ear.

It sounds like a Christmas pantomime; but when we remember that the French court, that model of patrician pride, was playing with democracy, with republicanism, with the simple life, as presented by Rousseau to its consideration, we see plainly enough how the real self-sufficiency of caste and the purely artificial sentiment of the day found expression in absurdities of costume. Women dared to wear such things, because, being aristocrats, they felt sure of themselves: and they professed to admire them, because, being engulfed in sentiment, they had lost all sense of proportion. A miller and his donkey were rustic (Marie Antoinette adored rusticity); an abbé flirting with a miller's wife was as obviously artificial as Watteau. It would have been hard to find a happier or more expressive combination. And when Rousseau and republicanism had won the race, we find the ladies of the Directoire illustrating the national illusions with clinging and diaphanous draperies; and asserting their affinity with the high ideals of ancient Greece by wearing sandals instead of shoes, and rings on their bare white toes. The reaction from the magnificent formalism of court dress to this abrupt nudity is in itself a record as graphic and as illuminating as anything that historians have to tell. The same great principle was at work in England when the Early Victorian virtues asserted their supremacy, when the fashionable world, becoming for a spell domestic and demure, expressed these qualities in smoothly banded hair, and draperies of decorous amplitude. There is, in fact, no phase of national life or national sentiment which has not betrayed itself to the world in dress.

And not national life only, but individual life as well. Clothes are more than historical, they are autobiographical. They tell their story in broad outlines and in minute detail. Was it for nothing that Charles the First devised that rich and sombre costume of black and white from which he never sought relief? Was it for nothing that Garibaldi wore a red shirt, and Napoleon an old grey coat? In proof that these things stood for character and destiny, we have but to look at the resolute but futile attempt which Charles the Second made to follow his father's lead, to express something beyond a fluctuating fashion in his dress. In 1666 he announced to his Council — which was, we trust, gratified by the intelligence — that he intended to wear one unaltered costume for the rest of his days. A month later he donned this costume, the distinguishing features of which were a long, close-fitting, black waistcoat, pinked with white, a loose embroidered surtout, and buskins. The court followed his example, and Charles not unnaturally complained that so many black and white waistcoats made him feel as though he were surrounded by magpies. So the white pinking was discarded, and plain black velvet waistcoats substituted. These were neither very gay, nor very becoming to a swarthy monarch; and the never-to-be-altered costume lasted less than two years, to the great relief of the courtiers, especially of those who had risked betting with the king himself on its speedy disappearance. Expressing nothing but a caprice, it had the futility and the impermanence of all caprices.

Within the last century, men have gradually, and it would seem permanently, abandoned the effort to reveal their personality in dress. They have allowed themselves to be committed for life to a costume of ruthless utilitarianism, which takes no count of physical beauty, or of its just display. Comfort, convenience, and sanitation have conspired to establish a rigidity of rule never seen before, to which men yield a docile and lamblike obedience. Robert Burton's axiom, "Nothing sooner dejects a man than clothes out of fashion," is as true now as it was three hundred years ago. Fashion sways the shape of a collar, and the infinitesimal gradations of a hat-brim; but the sense of fitness, and the power of interpreting life, which ennobled fashion in Burton's day, have disappeared in an enforced monotony.

Men take a strange perverted pride in this mournful sameness of attire, — delight in wearing a hat like every other man's hat, are content that it should be a perfected miracle of ugliness, that it should be hot, that it should be heavy, that it should be disfiguring, if only they can make sure of seeing fifty, or a hundred and fifty, other hats exactly like it on their way downtown. So absolute is this uniformity that the late Marquess of Ailesbury bore all his life a reputation for eccentricity, which seems to have had no other foundation than the fact of his wearing hats, or rather a hat, of distinctive shape, chosen with reference to his own head rather than to the heads of some odd millions of fellow citizens. The story is told of his standing bareheaded in a hatter's shop, awaiting the return of a salesman who had carried off his own beloved head-gear, when a short-sighted bishop entered, and, not recognizing the peer, took him for an assistant, and handed him *his* hat, asking him if he had any exactly like it. Lord Ailesbury turned the bishop's hat over and over, examined it carefully inside and out, and gave it back again. "No," he said, "I have n't, and I 'll be damned if I 'd wear it, if I had."

Even before the establishment of the invincible despotism which clothes the gentlemen of Christendom in a livery, we find the masculine mind disposed to severity in the ruling of fashions. Steele, for example, tells us the shocking story of an English gentleman who would persist in wearing a broad belt with a hanger, instead of the light sword then carried by men of rank, although in other respects he was a "perfectly well-bred person." Steele naturally regarded this acquaintance with deep suspicion, which was justified when, twenty-two years afterwards, the innovator married his cook-maid. "Others were amazed at this," writes the essayist, "but I must confess that I was not. I had always known that his deviation from the costume of a gentleman indicated an ill-balanced mind."

Now the adoption of a rigorous and monotonous utilitarianism in masculine attire has had two unlovely results. In the first place, men, since they ceased to covet beautiful clothes for themselves, have wasted much valuable time in counselling and censuring women; and, in the second place, there has come, with the loss of their fine trappings, a corresponding loss of illusions on the part of the women who look at them. Black broadcloth and derby hats are calculated to destroy the most robust illusions in Christendom; and men — from motives hard to fathom — have refused to retain in their wardrobes a single article which can amend an imperfect ideal. This does not imply that women fail to value friends in black broadcloth, nor that they refuse their affections to lovers and husbands in derby hats. Nature is not to be balked by such impediments. But as long as men wore costumes which interpreted their strength, enhanced their persuasiveness, and concealed their shortcomings, women accepted their dominance without demur. They made no idle claim to equality with creatures, not only bigger and stronger, not only more capable and more resolute, not only wiser and more experienced, but more noble and distinguished in appearance than they were themselves. What if the assertive attitude of the modern woman, her easy arrogance, and the confidence she places in her own untried powers, may be accounted for by the dispiriting clothes which men have determined to wear, and the wearing of which may have cost them no small portion of their authority?

The whole attitude of women in this regard is fraught with significance. Men have rashly discarded those details of costume which enhanced their comeliness and charm (we have but to look at Van Dyck's portraits to see how much rare distinction is traceable to subdued elegance of dress); but women have never through the long centuries laid aside the pleasant duty of self-adornment. They dare not if they would,—too much is at stake; and they experience the just delight which comes from coöperation with a natural law. The flexibility of their dress gives them every opportunity to modify, to enhance, to reveal, and to conceal. It is in the highest degree interpretative, and through it they express their aspirations and ideals, their thirst for combat and their realization of defeat, their fluctuating sentiments and their permanent predispositions.

> "A winning wave, deserving note,
> In the tempestuous petticoat;
> A careless shoe-string, in whose tie
> I see a wild civility."

Naturally, in a matter so vital, they are not disposed to listen to reason, and they cannot be argued out of a great fundamental instinct. Women are constitutionally incapable of being influenced by argument, — a limitation which is in the nature of a safeguard. The cunning words in which M. Marcel Provost urges them to follow the example of men, sounds, to their ears, a little like the words in which the fox which had lost its tail counsels its fellow foxes to rid themselves of so despicable an appendage. "Before the Revolution," writes M. Provost, in his "Lettres à François," "the clothes worn by men of quality were more costly than those worn by women. To-day all men dress with such uniformity that a Huron, transported to Paris or to London, could not distinguish master from valet. This will assuredly be the fate of feminine toilets in a future more or less near. The time must come when the varying costumes now seen at balls, at the races, at the theatre, will all be swept away; and in their place women will wear, as men do, a species of uniform. There will be a 'woman's suit,' costing sixty francs at Batignolles, and five hundred francs in the rue de la Paix; and, this reform once accomplished, it will never be possible to return to old conditions. Reason will have triumphed."

Perhaps! But reason has been routed

so often from the field that one no longer feels confident of her success. M. Baudrillart had a world of reason on his side when, before the Chamber of Deputies, he urged reform in dress, and the legal suppression of jewels and costly fabrics. M. de Lavaleye, the Belgian statist, was fortified by reason when he proposed his grey serge uniform for women of all classes. If we turn back a page or two of history, and look at the failure of the sumptuary laws in England, we find the wives of London tradesmen, who were not permitted to wear velvet in public, lining their grogram gowns with this costly fabric, for the mere pleasure of possession, for the meaningless — and most unreasonable — joy of expenditure. And when Queen Elizabeth, who considered extravagance in dress to be a royal prerogative, attempted to coerce the ladies of her court into simplicity, the Countess of Shrewsbury comments with ill-concealed irony on the result of such reasonable endeavours. "How often hath her majestie, with the grave advice of her honourable Councell, sette down the limits of apparell of every degree; and how soon again hath the pride of our harts overflown the chanell."

There are two classes of critics who still waste their vital forces in a futile attempt to reform feminine dress. The first class cherish artistic sensibilities which are grievously wounded by the caprices of fashion. They anathematize a civilization which tolerates ear-rings, or feathered hats, or artificial flowers. They appear to suffer vicarious torments from high-heeled shoes, spotted veils, and stays. They have occasional doubts as to the moral influence of ball-dresses. An unusually sanguine writer of this order has assured us, in the pages of the "Contemporary Review," that when women once assume their civic responsibilities, they will dress as austerely as men. The first fruits of the suffrage will be seen in sober and virtue-compelling gowns at the opera.

The second class of critics is made up of economists, who believe that too much of the world's earnings is spent upon clothes, and that this universal spirit of extravagance retards marriage, and blocks the progress of the race. It is in an ignoble effort to pacify these last censors that women writers undertake to tell their women readers, in the pages of women's periodicals, how to dress on sums of incredible insufficiency. Such misleading guides would be harmless, and even in their way amusing, if nobody believed them; but unhappily somebody always does believe them, and that somebody is too often a married man. There is no measure to the credulity of the average semi-educated man when confronted by a printed page (print carries such authority in his eyes), and with rows of figures, all showing conclusively that two and two make three, and that with economy and good management they can be reduced to one and a half. He has never mastered, and apparently never will master, the exact shade of difference between a statement and a fact.

Women are, under most circumstances, even more readily deceived; but, in the matter of dress, they have walked the thorny paths of experience. They know the cruel cost of everything they wear, — a cost which in this country is artificially maintained by a high protective tariff, — and they are not to be cajoled by that delusive word "simplicity," being too well aware that it is, when synonymous with good taste, the consummate success of artists, and the crowning achievement of wealth. Some years ago there appeared in one of the English magazines an article entitled, "How to Dress on Thirty Pounds a Year. As a Lady. By a Lady." Whereupon "Punch" offered the following light-minded amendment: "How to Dress on

Nothing a Year. As a Kaffir. By a Kaffir." At least a practical proposition.

Mr. Henry James has written some charming paragraphs on the symbolic value of clothes, as illustrated by the costumes worn by the French actresses of the Comédie, — women to whose unerring taste dress affords an expression of fine dramatic quality. He describes with enthusiasm the appearance of Madame Nathalie, when playing the part of an elderly provincial bourgeoise in a curtain-lifter called "Le Village."

"It was the quiet felicity of the old lady's dress that used to charm me. She wore a large black silk mantilla of a peculiar cut, which looked as if she had just taken it tenderly out of some old wardrobe where it lay folded in lavender, and a large dark bonnet, adorned with handsome black silk loops and bows. The extreme suggestiveness, and yet the taste and temperateness of this costume, seemed to me inimitable. The bonnet alone, with its handsome, decent, virtuous bows, was worth coming to see."

If we compare this "quiet felicity" of the artist with the absurd travesties worn on our American stage, we can better understand the pleasure which filled Mr. James's heart. What, for example, would Madame Nathalie have thought of the modish gowns which Mrs. Fiske introduces into the middle-class Norwegian life of Ibsen's dramas? No plays can less well bear such inaccuracies, because they depend on their stage-setting to bring before our eyes their alien aspect, to make us feel an atmosphere with which we are wholly unfamiliar. The accessories are few, but of supreme importance; and it is inconceivable that a keenly intelligent actress like Mrs. Fiske should sacrifice *vraisemblance* to a meaningless refinement. In the second act of "Rosmersholm," to take a single instance, the text calls for a morning wrapper, a thing so manifestly careless and informal that the school-master, Kroll, is scandalized at seeing Rebecca in it, and says so plainly. But as Mrs. Fiske plays the scene in a tea-gown of elaborate elegance, in which she might with propriety have received the Archbishop of Canterbury, Kroll's studied apologies for intruding upon her before she has had time to dress, and the whole suggestion of undue intimacy between Rebecca and Rosmer, which Ibsen meant to convey, is irrevocably lost. And to weaken a situation for the sake of being prettily dressed would be impossible to a French actress, trained in the delicacies of her art.

If the feeling for clothes, the sense of their correspondence with time and place, with public enthusiasms and with private sensibilities, has always belonged to France, it was a no less dominant note in Italy during the two hundred years in which she eclipsed and bewildered the rest of Christendom; and it bore fruit in those great historic wardrobes which the Italian chroniclers describe with loving minuteness. We know all about Isabella d' Este's gowns, as if she had worn them yesterday. We know all about the jewels which were the assertion of her husband's pride in times of peace, and his security with the Lombard bankers in times of war. We know what costumes the young Beatrice d' Este carried with her on her mission to Venice, and how favourably they impressed the grave Venetian Senate. We can count the shifts in Lucretia Borgia's trousseau, when that much-slandered woman became Duchess of Ferrara, and we can reckon the cost of the gold fringe which hung from her linen sleeves. We are told which of her robes was wrought with fish scales, and which with interlacing leaves, and which with a hem of pure and flame-like gold. Ambassadors described in state papers her green velvet cap with its golden ornaments, and the emerald she wore on her forehead, and the black ribbon which tied her beautiful fair hair.

These vanities harmonized with character and circumstance. The joy of living was then expressing itself in an overwhelming sense of beauty, and in material splendour which, unlike the material splendour of to-day, never overstepped the standard set by the intellect. Taste had become a triumphant principle, and as women grew in dignity and importance, they set a higher and higher value on the compelling power of dress. They had no more doubt on this score than had wise Homer when he hung the necklaces around Aphrodite's tender neck before she was well out of the sea, winding them row after row in as many circles as there are stars clustering about the moon. No more doubt than had the fair and virtuous Countess of Salisbury, who, so Froissart tells us, chilled the lawless passion of Edward the Third by the simple expedient of wearing unbefitting clothes.

Saint Lucy, under somewhat similar circumstances, felt it necessary to put out her beautiful eyes; but Katharine of Salisbury knew men better than the saint knew them. She shamed her loveliness by going to Edward's banquet looking like a rustic, and found herself in consequence very comfortably free from royal attentions.

In the wise old days when men outshone their consorts, we find their hearts set discerningly on one supreme extravagance. Lace, the most artistic fabric that taste and ingenuity have devised, "the fine web which feeds the pride of the world," was for centuries the delight of every well-dressed gentleman. We know not by what marital cajolery Mr. Pepys persuaded Mrs. Pepys to give him the lace from her best petticoat, "that she had when I married her"; but we do know that he used it to trim a new coat; and that he subsequently noted down in his diary one simple, serious, and heartfelt resolution, which we feel sure was faithfully kept: "Henceforth I am determined my chief expense shall be in lace bands." Charles the Second paid fifteen pounds apiece for his lace-trimmed night-caps; William the Third, five hundred pounds for a set of lace-trimmed night-shirts; and Cinq-Mars, the favourite of Louis the Thirteenth, who was beheaded when he was barely twenty-two, found time in his short life to acquire three hundred sets of lace ruffles. The lace collars of Van Dyck's portraits, the lace cravats which Grahame of Claverhouse and Montrose wear over their armour, are subtly suggestive of the strength that lies in delicacy. The fighting qualities of Claverhouse were not less effective because of those soft folds of lace and linen. The death of Montrose was no less noble because he went to the scaffold in scarlet and fine linen, with "stockings of incarnate silk, and roses on his shoon." Once Carlyle was disparaging Montrose, as (being in a denunciatory mood) he would have disparaged the Archangel Michael; and, finding his hearers disposed to disagree with him, asked bitterly: "What did Montrose do anyway?" Whereupon Irving retorted: "He put on a clean shirt to be hanged in, and that is more than you, Carlyle, would ever have done in his place."

It was the association of the scaffold with an ignoble victim which banished black satin from the London world. Because a foul-hearted murderess[1] elected to be hanged in this material, Englishwomen refused for years to wear it, and many bales of black satin languished on the drapers' shelves, —a memorable instance of the significance which attaches itself to dress. The caprices of fashion do more than illustrate a woman's capacity or incapacity for selection. They mirror her inward refinements, and symbolize those feminine virtues and vani-

[1] Mrs. Manning.

ties which are so closely akin as to be occasionally undistinguishable.

"A saint in crape is twice a saint in lawn,"

mocked Pope; and woman smiles at the satire, knowing more about the matter than Pope could ever have known, and seeing a little sparkle of truth glimmering beneath the gibe. Fashion fluctuates from one charming absurdity to another, and each in turn is welcomed and dismissed; through each in turn woman endeavours to reveal her own elusive personality. Poets no longer praise with Herrick the brave vibrations of her petticoats. Ambassadors no longer describe her caps and ribbons in their official documents. Novelists no longer devote twenty pages, as did the admirable Richardson, to the wedding finery of their heroines. Men have ceased to be vitally interested in dress, but none the less are they sensitive to its influence and enslaved by its results; while women, preserving through the centuries the great traditions of their sex, still rate at its utmost value the prize for which Eve sold her freehold in the Garden of Paradise.

"The Greatest of These is Charity"

Mrs. James Gordon Harrington Balderston to Mrs. Lapham Shepherd

MY DEAR MRS. SHEPHERD,
Will you pardon me for this base encroachment on your time? Busy women are the only ones who ever *have* any time, so the rest of the world is forced to steal from them. And then all that you organize is so successful that every one turns naturally to you for advice and assistance, as I am turning now. A really charming woman, a Miss Alexandrina Ramsay, who has lived for years in Italy, is anxious to give a series of lectures on Dante. I am sure they will be interesting, for she can put so much local colour into them, and I un-

derstand she is a fluent Italian scholar. Her uncle was the English Consul in Florence or Naples, I don't remember which, so she has had unusual opportunities for study; and her grandfather was Dr. Alexander Ramsay, who wrote a history of the Hebrides. Unfortunately her voice is not very strong, so she would be heard to the best advantage in a drawing-room. I am wondering whether you would consent to lend yours, which is so beautiful, or whether you could put Miss Ramsay in touch with the Century Club, or the Spalding School. You will find her attractive, I am sure. The Penhursts knew her well in Munich, and have given her a letter to me.

Pray allow me to congratulate you on your new honours as a grandmother. I trust that both your daughter and the baby are well.

Very sincerely yours,

IRENE BALDERSTON.

I forgot to tell you that Miss Ramsay's lectures are on

Dante, the Lover.
Dante, the Poet.
Dante, the Patriot.
Dante, the Reformer.

There was a fifth on Dante, the Prophet, but I persuaded her to leave it out of the course.

I. B.

Mrs. Lapham Shepherd to Mrs. Wilfred Ward Hamilton

DEAR MRS. HAMILTON, —

Mrs. James Balderston has asked me to do what I can for a Miss Alexandrina Ramsay (granddaughter of the historian), who wants to give four lectures on Dante in Philadelphia. She has chopped him up into poet, prophet, lover, etc. I cannot have any lectures or readings in my house this winter. Jane is still far from strong, and we shall probably go South after Christmas. Please don't let me put any burden on your shoulders; but if Dr. Hamilton could persuade those nice Quakers at Swarthmore that there is nothing so educational as a course of Dante, it would be the best possible opening for Miss Ramsay. Mrs. Balderston seems to think her voice would not carry in a large room, but as students never listen to anybody, this would make very little difference. The Century Club has been suggested, but I fancy the classes there have been arranged for the season. There are preparatory schools, are n't there, at Swarthmore, which need to know about Dante? Or would there be any chance at all at Miss Irington's?

Miss Ramsay has been to see me, and I feel sorry for the girl. Her uncle was the English Consul at Milan, and the poor thing loved Italy (who does n't!), and hated to leave it. I wish she could establish herself as a lecturer, though there is nothing I detest more ardently than lectures.

I missed you sorely at the meeting of the Aubrey Home house-committee yesterday. Harriet Maline and Mrs. Percy Brown had a battle royal over the laying of the new water-pipes, and over *my* prostrate body, which still aches from the contest. I wish Harriet would resign. She is the only creature I have ever known, except the Bate's parrot and my present cook, who is perpetually out of temper. If she were not my husband's stepmother's niece, I am sure I could stand up to her better.

Cordially yours,
ALICE LEIGH SHEPHERD.

Mrs. Wilfred Ward Hamilton to Miss Violet Wray

DEAR VIOLET, —

You know Margaret Irington better than I do. Do you think she would like to have a course of Dante in her school this winter? A very clever and charming woman, a Miss Alexandrina Ramsay, has four lectures on the poet which she is anxious to give before schools, or clubs, or — if she can — in private houses. I have promised Mrs. Shepherd to do anything in my power to help her. It occurred to me that the Contemporary Club might like to have one of the lectures, and you are on the committee. That would be the making of Miss Ramsay, if only she could be heard in that huge Clover Room. I understand she has a pleasant cultivated voice, but is not accustomed to public speaking. There must be plenty of smaller clubs at Bryn Mawr, or Haverford, or Chestnut Hill, for which she would be just the thing. Her grandfather wrote a history of England, and I have a vague impression that I studied it at school. I should write to the Drexel Institute, but don't know anybody connected with it. Do you? It would be a real kindness to give Miss Ramsay a start, and I know you do not begrudge trouble in a good cause. You did such wonders for Fräulein Breitenbach last winter.

Love to your mother,

Affectionately yours,
HANNAH GALE HAMILTON.

Miss Violet Wray to Mrs. J. Lockwood Smith

DEAR ANN, —

I have been requested by Hannah Hamilton — may Heaven forgive her! — to find lecture engagements for a Miss Ramsay, Miss Alexandrina Ramsay, who wants to tell the American public what she knows about Dante. Why a Scotchwoman should be turned loose in the Inferno, I cannot say; but it seems her father or her grandfather wrote school-books, and she is carrying on the educational traditions of the family. Hannah made the unholy suggestion that she should speak at the Contemporary Club, and offered as an inducement the fact that she could n't be heard in so large a room. But we are supposed to discuss topics of the day, and Dante happened some little while ago. He has no bearing upon aviation, or National Insurance Bills (that is our subject next Monday night); but he is brimming over with ethics, and it is the duty of your precious Ethical Society to grapple with him exhaustively. I always wondered what took you to that strange substitute for church; but now I see in it the hand of Providence pointing the way to Miss Ramsay's lecture field. Please persuade your fellow Ethicals that four lectures—or even one lecture—on Dante will be what Alice Hunt calls an "uplift." I feel that I must try and find an opening for Hannah's protégée, because she helped me with Fräulein Breitenbach's concert last winter,—a circumstance she does not lightly permit me to forget. Did I say, "May Heaven forgive her" for saddling me with this Scotch schoolmaster's daughter? Well, I take back that devout supplication. May jackals sit on her grandmother's grave! Meantime here is Miss Ramsay to be provided for. If your Ethicals (disregarding their duty) will have none of her, please think up somebody with a taste for serious study, and point out that Dante, elucidated by a Scotchwoman, will probably be as serious as anything that has visited Philadelphia since the yellow fever.

If you want one of Grisette's kittens, there are still two left. The handsomest of all has gone to live in regal splendour at the Bruntons, and I have promised another to our waitress who was married last month. Such are the vicissitudes of life.

Ever yours,

VIOLET WRAY.

Mrs. J. Lockwood Smith to Mrs. James Gordon Harrington Balderston

DEAR MRS. BALDERSTON, —

I want to enlist your interest in a clever

young Scotchwoman, a Miss Alexandrina Ramsay, who hopes to give four lectures on Dante in Philadelphia this winter. Her father was an eminent teacher in his day, and I understand she is thoroughly equipped for her work. Heaven knows I wish fewer lecturers would cross the sea to enlighten our ignorance, and so will you when you get this letter; but I remember with what enthusiasm you talked about Italy and Dante at Brown's Mills last spring, and I trust that your ardour has not waned. The Century Club seems to me the best possible field for Miss Ramsay. Do you know any one on the entertainment committee, and do you think it is not too late in the season to apply? Of course there are always the schools. Dear Mrs. Balderston, I should feel more shame in troubling you, did I not know how capable you are, and how much weight your word carries. Violet Wray and Mrs. Wilfred Hamilton are tremendously interested in Miss Ramsay.

May I tell Violet to send her to you, so that you can see for yourself what she is like, and what chances she has of success? Please be quite frank in saying yes or no, and believe me always,

Yours very cordially,

ANN HAZELTON SMITH.

The Customary Correspondent

"Letters warmly sealed and coldly opened."
RICHTER.

WHY do so many ingenious theorists give fresh reasons every year for the decline of letter writing, and why do they assume, in derision of suffering humanity, that it has declined? They lament the lack of leisure, the lack of sentiment, — Mr. Lucas adds the lack of stamps, — which chill the ardour of the correspondent; and they fail to ascertain how chilled he is, or how far he sets at naught these justly restraining influences. They talk of telegrams, and telephones, and postal cards, as if any discovery of science, any device of civilization, could eradicate from the human heart that passion for self-expression which is the impelling force of letters. They also fail to note that, side by side with telephones and telegrams, comes the baleful reduction of postage rates, which lowers our last barrier of defence. Two cents an ounce leaves us naked at the mercy of the world.

It is on record that a Liverpool tradesman once wrote to Dickens, to express the pleasure he had derived from that great Englishman's immortal novels, and enclosed, by way of testimony, a cheque for five hundred pounds. This is a phenomenon which ought to be more widely known than it is, for there is no natural law to prevent its recurrence; and while the world will never hold another Dickens, there are many deserving novelists who may like to recall the incident when they open their morning's mail. It would be pleasant to associate our morning's mail with such fair illusions; and though writing to strangers is but a parlous pastime, the Liverpool gentleman threw a new and radiant light upon its possibilities. "The gratuitous contributor is, *ex vi termini*, an ass," said Christopher North sourly; but then he never knew, nor ever deserved to know, this particular kind of contribution.

Generally speaking, the unknown correspondent does not write to praise. His guiding principle is the diffusion of useless knowledge, and he demands or imparts it according to the exigencies of the hour. It is strange that a burning thirst for information should be combined with such reluctance to acquire it through ordinary channels. A man who wishes to write a paper on the botanical value of Shakespeare's plays does not dream of consulting a concordance and a botany, and then going to work. The bald simplicity of such a process offends his sense of magnitude. He writes to a distinguished scholar, asking a number of burdensome questions, and is apparently under the impression that the resources of the scholar's mind, the fruits of boundless industry, should be cheerfully placed at his disposal. A woman who meditates a "literary essay" upon domestic pets is not content to track her quarry through the long library shelves. She writes to some painstaking worker, enquiring what English poets have "sung the praises of the cat," and if Cowper was the only author who ever domesticated hares? One of Huxley's most amusing letters is written in reply to a gentleman who wished to compile an article on "Home Pets of Celebrities," and who unhesitatingly applied for particulars concerning the Hodeslea cat.

These are, of course, labour-saving devices, but economy of effort is not always the ambition of the correspondent. It would seem easier, on the whole, to open a dictionary of quotations than to compose an elaborately polite letter, requesting to know who said—

"Fate cannot harm me; I have dined to-day."

It is certainly easier, and far more agreeable, to read Charles Lamb's essays than to ask a stranger in which one of them he discovered the author's heterodox views on encyclopædias. It involves no great fatigue to look up a poem of Herrick's, or a letter of Shelley's, or a novel of Peacock's (these things are accessible and repay enquiry), and it would be a rational and self-respecting thing to do, instead of endeavouring to extort information (like an intellectual footpad) from writers who are in no way called upon to furnish it.

One thing is sure. As long as there are people in this world whose guiding principle is the use of other people's brains, there can be no decline and fall of letter-writing. The correspondence which plagued our great-grandfathers a hundred years ago, plagues their descendants to-day. Readers of Lockhart's "Scott" will remember how an Edinburgh minister named Brunton, who wished to compile a hymnal, wrote to the poet Crabbe for a list of hymns; and how Crabbe (who, albeit a clergyman, knew probably as little about hymns as any man in England) wrote in turn to Scott, to please help him to help Brunton; and how Scott replied in desperation that he envied the hermit of Prague who never saw pen nor ink. How many of us have in our day thought longingly of that blessed anchorite! Surely Mr. Herbert Spencer must, consciously or unconsciously, have shared Scott's sentiments, when he wrote a letter to the public press, explaining with patient courtesy that, being old, and busy, and very tired, it was no longer possible for him to answer all the unknown correspondents who demanded information upon every variety of subject. He had tried to do this for many years, but the tax was too heavy for his strength, and he was compelled to take refuge in silence.

Ingenious authors and editors who

ask for free copy form a class apart. They are not pursuing knowledge for their own needs, but offering themselves as channels through which we may gratuitously enlighten the world. Their questions, though intimate to the verge of indiscretion, are put in the name of humanity; and we are bidden to confide to the public how far we indulge in the use of stimulants, what is the nature of our belief in immortality, if — being women — we should prefer to be men, and what incident of our lives has most profoundly affected our careers. Reticence on our part is met by the assurance that eminent people all over the country are hastening to answer these queries, and that the "unique nature" of the discussion will make it of permanent value to mankind. We are also told in soothing accents that our replies need not exceed a few hundred words, as the editor is nobly resolved not to infringe upon our valuable time.

Less commercial, but quite as importunate, are the correspondents who belong to literary societies, and who have undertaken to read, before these select circles, papers upon every conceivable subject, from the Bride of the Canticle to the divorce laws of France. They regret their own ignorance — as well they may — and blandly ask for aid. There is no limit to demands of this character. The young Englishwoman who wrote to Tennyson, requesting some verses which she might read as her own at a picnic, was not more intrepid than the American school-girl who recently asked a man of letters to permit her to see an unpublished address, as she had heard that it dealt with the subject of her graduation paper, and hoped it might give her some points. It is hard to believe that the timidity natural to youth — or which we used to think natural to youth — could be so easily overcome; or that the routine of school work, which makes for honest if inefficient acquirements, could leave a student still begging or borrowing her way.

We must in justice admit, however, that the unknown correspondent is as ready to volunteer assistance as to demand it. He is ingenious in criticism, and fertile in suggestions. He has inspirations in the way of plots and topics, — like that amiable baronet, Sir John Sinclair, who wanted Scott to write a poem on the adventures and intrigues of a Caithness mermaiden, and who proffered him, by way of inducement, "all the information I possess." The correspondent's tone, when writing to humbler drudges in the field, is kind and patronizing. He admits that he likes your books, or at least — here is a veiled reproach — that he "has liked the earlier ones"; he assumes, unwarrantably, that you are familiar with his favourite authors; and he believes that it would be for you "an interesting and congenial task" to trace the "curious connection" between American fiction and the stock exchange. Sometimes, with thinly veiled sarcasm, he demands that you should "enlighten his dulness," and say *why* you gave your book its title. If he cannot find a French word you have used in his "excellent dictionary," he thinks it worth while to write and tell you so. He fears you do not "wholly understand or appreciate the minor poets of your native land"; and he protests, more in sorrow than in anger, against certain innocent phrases with which you have disfigured "your otherwise graceful pages."

Now it must be an impulse not easily resisted which prompts people to this gratuitous expression of their opinions. They take a world of trouble which they could so easily escape; they deem it their privilege to break down the barriers which civilization has taught us to respect; and if they ever find themselves repaid, it is assuredly by something remote from the gratitude of their correspondents. Take, for example, the case of Mr. Peter Bayne, journalist, and biographer of Martin Luther, who wrote to Tennyson, — with whom he was unacquainted, — protesting earnestly against a line in "Lady Clare": —

"'If I'm a beggar born,' she said."

It was Mr. Bayne's opinion that such an expression was not only exaggerated, inasmuch as the nurse was not, and never had been, a beggar; but, coming from a child to her mother, was harsh and unfilial. "The criticism of my heart," he wrote, "tells me that Lady Clare could never have said that."

Tennyson was perhaps the last man in Christendom to have accepted the testimony of Mr. Bayne's heart-throbs. He intimated with some asperity that he knew better than any one else what Lady Clare *did* say, and he pointed out that she had just cause for resentment against a mother who had placed her in such an embarrassing position. The controversy is one of the drollest in literature; but what is hard to understand is the mental attitude of a man — and a reasonably busy man — who could attach so much importance to Lady Clare's remarks, and who could feel himself justified in correcting them.

Begging letters form a class apart. They represent a great and growing industry, and they are too purposeful to illustrate the abstract passion for correspondence. Yet marvellous things have been done in this field. There is an ingenuity, a freshness and fertility of device about the begging letter which lifts it often to the realms of genius. Experienced though we all are, it has surprises in store for every one of us. Seasoned though we are, we cannot read without appreciation of its more daring and fantastic flights. There was, for instance, a very imperative person who wrote to

Dickens for a donkey, and who said he would call for it the next day, as though Dickens kept a herd of donkeys in Tavistock Square, and could always spare one for an emergency. There was a French gentleman who wrote to Moore, demanding a lock of Byron's hair for a young lady, who would — so he said — die if she did not get it. This was a very lamentable letter, and Moore was conjured, in the name of the young lady's distracted family, to send the lock, and save her from the grave. And there was a misanthrope who wrote to Peel that he was weary of the ways of men (as so, no doubt, was Peel), and who requested a hermitage in some nobleman's park, where he might live secluded from the world. The best begging-letter writers depend upon the element of surprise as a valuable means to their end. I knew a benevolent old lady who, in 1885, was asked to subscribe to a fund for the purchase of "moderate luxuries" for the

French soldiers in Madagascar. "What did you do?" I asked, when informed of the incident. "I sent the money," was the placid reply. "I thought I might never again have an opportunity to send money to Madagascar."

It would be idle to deny that a word of praise, a word of thanks, sometimes a word of criticism, have been powerful factors in the lives of men of genius. We know how profoundly Lord Byron was affected by the letter of a consumptive girl, written simply and soberly, signed with initials only, seeking no notice and giving no address; but saying in a few candid words that the writer wished before she died to thank the poet for the rapture his poems had given her. "I look upon such a letter," wrote Byron to Moore, "as better than a diploma from Göttingen." We know, too, what a splendid impetus to Carlyle was that first letter from Goethe, a letter which he confessed seemed too wonderful to be real, and more "like a message from fairyland." It was but a brief note after all, tepid, sensible, and egotistical; but the magic sentence, "It may be I shall yet hear much of you," became for years an impelling force, the kind of prophecy which insured its own fulfilment.

Carlyle was susceptible to praise, though few readers had the temerity to offer it. We find him, after the publication of the "French Revolution," writing urbanely to a young and unknown admirer; "I do not blame your enthusiasm." But when a less happily-minded youth sent him some suggestions for the reformation of society, Carlyle, who could do all his own grumbling, returned his disciple's complaints with this laconic denial: "A pack of damned nonsense, you unfortunate fool." It sounds unkind; but we must remember that there were six posts a day in London, that "each post brought its batch of letters," and that nine tenths of these letters — so Carlyle says — were from strangers, demanding autographs, and seeking or proffering advice. One man wrote that he was distressingly ugly, and asked what should he do about it. "So profitable have my epistolary fellow creatures grown to me in these years," notes the historian in his journal, "that when the postman leaves nothing, it may well be felt as an escape."

The most patient correspondent known to fame was Sir Walter Scott, though Lord Byron surprises us at times by the fine quality of his good nature. His letters are often petulant, — especially when Murray has sent him tragedies instead of tooth-powder; but he is perhaps the only man on record who received with perfect equanimity the verses of an aspiring young poet, wrote him the cheerfullest of letters, and actually invited him to breakfast. The letter is still extant; but the verses were so little the precursor of fame that the youth's subsequent history is to this day unknown. It was with truth that Byron said of himself: "I am really a civil and polite person, and do hate pain when it can be avoided."

Scott was also civil and polite, and his heart beat kindly for every species of bore. As a consequence, the world bestowed its tediousness upon him, to the detriment of his happiness and health. Ingenious jokers translated his verses into Latin, and then wrote to accuse him of plagiarizing from Vida. Proprietors of patent medicines offered him fabulous sums to link his fame with theirs. Modest ladies proposed that he should publish their effusions as his own, and share the profits. Poets demanded that he should find publishers for their epics, and dramatists that he should find managers for their plays. Critics pointed out to him his anachronisms, and well-intentioned readers set him right on points of morality and law. When he was old, and ill, and ruined, there was yet no respite from the curse of correspondents. A year before his death he wrote dejectedly in his journal:—"A fleece of letters which must be answered, I suppose; all from persons—my zealous admirers, of course—who expect me to make up whatever losses have been their lot, raise them to a desirable rank, and stand their protector and patron. I must, they take it for granted, be astonished at having an address from a stranger. On the contrary, I should be astonished if one of these extravagant epistles came from anybody who had the least title to enter into correspondence."

And there are people who believe, or who pretend to believe, that fallen human nature can be purged and amended by half-rate telegrams, and a telephone ringing in the hall. Rather let us abandon illusions, and echo Carlyle's weary cry, when he heard the postman knocking at his door: "Just Heavens! Does literature lead to this!"

The Benefactor

"He is a good man who can receive a gift well."
— EMERSON.

THERE is a sacredness of humility in such an admission which wins pardon for all the unlovely things which Emerson has crowded into a few pages upon "Gifts." Recognizing that his own goodness stopped short of this exalted point, he pauses for a moment in his able and bitter self-defence to pay tribute to a generosity he is too honest to claim. After all, who but Charles Lamb ever *did* receive gifts well? Scott tried, to be sure. No man ever sinned less than he against the law of kindness. But Lamb did not need to try. He had it in his heart of gold to feel pleasure in the presents which his friends took pleasure in giving him. The character and quality of the gifts were not determining factors. We cannot analyze this disposition. We can only admire it from afar.

"I look upon it as a point of morality to be obliged to those who endeavour to oblige me," says Sterne; and the sentiment, like most of Sterne's sentiments, is remarkably graceful. It has all the freshness of a principle never fagged out by practice. The rugged fashion in which Emerson lived up to his burdensome ideals prompted him to less engaging utterances. "It is not the office of a man to receive gifts," he writes viciously. "How dare you give them? We wish to be self-sustained. We do not quite forgive a giver. The hand that feeds us is in some danger of being bitten."

Carlyle is almost as disquieting. He searches for, and consequently finds, unworthy feelings both in the man who gives, and holds himself to be a benefactor, and in the man who receives, and burdens himself with a sense of obligation. He professes a stern dislike for presents, fearing lest they should undermine his moral stability; but a man so up in morals must have been well aware that he ran no great risk of parting with his stock in trade. He probably hated getting what he did not want, and finding himself expected to be grateful for it. This is a sentiment common to lesser men than Carlyle, and as old as the oldest gift-bearer. It has furnished food for fables, inspiration for satirists, and cruel stories at which the light-hearted laugh. Mr. James Payn used to tell the tale of an advocate who unwisely saved a client from the gallows which he should have graced; and the man, inspired by the best of motives, sent his benefactor from the West Indies a case of pineapples in which a colony of centipedes had bred so generously that they routed every servant from the unfortunate lawyer's house, and dwelt hideously and permanently in his kitchen. "A purchase is cheaper than a gift," says a wily old Italian proverb, steeped in the wisdom of the centuries.

The principle which prompts the selection of gifts — since selected they all are by some one — is for the most part a mystery. I never but once heard any reasonable solution, and that was volunteered by an old lady who had been listening in silence to a conversation on the engrossing subject of Christmas presents. It was a conversation at once animated and depressing. The time was at hand when none of us could hope to escape these tokens of regard, and the elaborate and ingenious character of their unfitness was frankly and fairly discussed. What baffled us was the theory of choice. Suddenly the old lady flooded this dark problem with light by observing that she always purchased her presents at bazaars. She said she knew they were useless, and that nobody wanted them, but that she considered it her duty to help the bazaars. She had the air of one conscious of well-doing, and sure of her reward. It did not seem to occur to her that the reward should, in justice, be passed on with the purchases. The necessities of charitable organizations called for a sacrifice, and, rising to the emergency, she sacrificed her friends.

A good many years have passed over our heads since Thackeray launched his invectives at the Christmas tributes he held in heartiest hatred, — the books which every season brought in its train, and which were never meant to be read. Their mission was fulfilled when they were sent by aunt to niece, by uncle to nephew, by friend to hapless friend. They were "gift-books" in the exclusive sense of the word. Thackeray was wont to declare that these vapid, brightly bound volumes played havoc with the happy homes of England, just as the New Year bonbons played havoc with the homes of France. Perhaps, of the two countries, France suffered less. The candy soon disappeared, leaving only impaired digestions in its wake. The books remained to encumber shelves, and bore humanity afresh.

> "*Moi, je dis que les bonbons*
> *Valent mieux que la raison*";

and they are at least less permanently oppressive. "When thou makest presents," said old John Fuller, "let them be of such things as will last long; to the end that they may be in some sort immortal, and may frequently refresh the memory of the receiver." But this excellent advice — excellent for the simple and spacious age in which it was written — presupposes the "immortal" presents to wear well. Theologians teach us that immortality is not necessarily a blessing.

A vast deal of ingenuity is wasted every year in evoking the undesirable, in the careful construction of objects which burden life. Frankenstein was a large rather than an isolated example.

The civilized world so teems with elaborate and unlovely inutilities, with things which seem foreign to any reasonable conditions of existence, that we are sometimes disposed to envy the savage who wears all his simple wardrobe without being covered, and who sees all his simple possessions in a corner of his empty hut. What pleasant spaces meet the savage eye! What admirable vacancies soothe the savage soul! No embroidered bag is needed to hold his sponge or his slippers. No painted box is destined for his postal cards. No decorated tablet waits for his laundry list. No ornate wall-pocket yawns for his unpaid bills. He smokes without cigarette-cases. He dances without cotillion favours. He enjoys all rational diversions, unfretted by the superfluities with which we have weighted them. Life, notwithstanding its pleasures, remains endurable to him.

Above all, he does not undermine his own moral integrity by vicarious benevolence, by helping the needy at his friend's expense. The great principle of giving away what one does not want to keep is probably as familiar to the savage as to his civilized, or semi-civilized brother. That vivacious traveller, Père Huc, tells us he has seen a Tartar chief at dinner gravely hand over to an underling a piece of gristle he found himself unable to masticate, and that the gift was received with every semblance of gratitude and delight. But there is a simple straightforwardness about an act like this which commends it to our understanding. The Tartar did not assume the gristle to be palatable. He did not veil his motives for parting with it. He did not expand with the emotions of a philanthropist. And he did not expect the Heavens to smile upon his deed.

One word must be said in behalf of the punctilious giver, of the man who repays a gift as scrupulously as he returns a blow. He wants to please, but he is baffled by not knowing, and by not being sympathetic enough to divine, what his inarticulate friend desires. And if he does know, he may still vacillate between his friend's sense of the becoming and his own. The "Spectator," in a mood of unwonted subtlety, tells us that there is a "mild treachery" in giving what we feel to be bad, because we are aware that the recipient will think it very good. If, for example, we hold garnets to be ugly and vulgar, we must not send them to a friend who considers them rich and splendid. "A gift should represent common ground."

This is so well said that it sounds like the easy thing it is n't. Which of us has not nobly striven, and ignobly failed, to preserve our honest purpose without challenging the taste of our friends? It is hard to tell what people really prize. Heine begged for a button from George Sand's trousers, and who shall say whether enthusiasm or malice prompted the request? Mr. Oscar Browning, who as Master at Eton must have known whereof he spoke, insisted that it was a mistake to give a boy a well-bound book if you expected him to read it. Yet binding plays a conspicuous part in the selection of Christmas and birthday presents. Dr. Johnson went a step farther, and said that nobody wanted to read *any* book which was given to him; — the mere fact that it was given, instead of being bought, borrowed, or ravished from a friend's shelves, militated against its readable qualities. Perhaps the Doctor was thinking of authors' copies. Otherwise the remark is the most discouraging one on record.

Yet when all the ungracious things have been said and forgotten, when the hard old proverbs have exhausted their unwelcome wisdom, and we have smiled wearily over the deeper cynicisms of Richelieu and Talleyrand, where shall we turn for relief but to Emerson, who has atoned in his own fashion for the harshness of his own words. It is not only that he recognizes the goodness of the man who receives a gift well; but he sees, and sees clearly, that there can be no question between friends of giving or receiving, no possible room for generosity or gratitude. "The gift to be true must be the flowing of the giver unto me, correspondent to my flowing unto him. When the waters are at a level, then my goods pass to him, and his to me. All his are mine, all mine, his."

Critics have been disposed to think that this is an elevation too lofty for plain human beings to climb, an air too rarified for them to breathe; and that it ill befitted a man who churlishly resented the simple, stupid kindnesses of life, to take so sublime a tone, to claim so fine a virtue. We cannot hope to scale great moral heights by ignoring petty obligations.

Yet Emerson does not go a step beyond Plato in his conception of the "level waters" of friendship. He states his position lucidly, and with a rational understanding of all that it involves. His vision is wide enough to embrace its everlasting truth. Plato says the same thing in simpler language. He offers his truth as self-evident, and in no need of demonstration. When Lysis and Menexenus greet Socrates at the gymnasia, the philosopher asks which of the two youths is the elder.

"'That,' said Menexenus, 'is a matter of dispute between us.'

"'And which is the nobler? Is that also a matter of dispute?'

"'Yes, certainly.'

"'And another disputed point is which is the fairer?'

"The two boys laughed.

"'I shall not ask which is the richer, for you are friends, are you not?'

"'We are friends.'

"'And friends have all things in common, so that one of you can be no richer than the other, if you say truly that you are friends.'

"They assented, and at that moment Menexenus was called away by some one who came and said that the master of the gymnasia wanted him." [1]

This is all. To Plato's way of thinking, the situation explained itself. The two boys could not share their beauty nor their strength, but money was a thing to pass from hand to hand. It was not, and it never could be, a matter for competition. The last lesson taught an Athenian youth was the duty of outstripping his neighbour in the hard race for wealth.

And where shall we turn for a practical illustration of friendship, as conceived by Emerson and Plato? Where shall we see the level waters, the "mine is thine" which we think too exalted for plain living? No need to search far, and no need to search amid the good and great. It is

[1] Lysis. Translated by Jowett.

a pleasure to find what we seek in the annals of the flagrantly sinful, of that notorious Duke of Queensberry, "Old Q," who has been so liberally and justly censured by Wordsworth and Burns, by Leigh Hunt and Sir George Trevelyan, and who was, in truth, gamester, roué, — and friend. In the last capacity he was called upon to listen to the woes of George Selwyn, who, having lost at Newmarket more money than he could possibly hope to pay, saw ruin staring him in the face. There is in Selwyn's letter a note of eloquent misery. He was, save when lulled to sleep in Parliament, a man of many words. There is in the letter of Lord March (he had not yet succeeded to the Queensberry title and estates) nothing but a quiet exposition of Plato's theory of friendship. Selwyn's debts and his friend's money are intercommunicable. The amount required has been placed that morning at the banker's. "I depend more," writes Lord March, "upon the continuance of our friendship than upon anything else in the world, because I have so many reasons to know you, and I am sure I know myself. *There will be no bankruptcy without we are bankrupt together.*"

Here are the waters flowing on a level, flowing between two men of the world; one of them great enough to give, without deeming himself a benefactor, and the other good enough to receive a gift well.

The Condescension of Borrowers

"Il n'est si riche qui quelquefois ne doibve. Il n'est si pauvre de qui quelquefois on ne puisse emprunter." —*Pantagruel.*

I LENT my umbrella," said my friend, "to my cousin, Maria. I was compelled to lend it to her because she could not, or would not, leave my house in the rain without it. I had need of that umbrella, and I tried to make it as plain as the amenities of language permitted that I expected to have it returned. Maria said superciliously that she hated to see other people's umbrellas littering the house, which gave me a gleam of hope. Two months later I found my property in the hands of her ten-year-old son, who was being marshalled with his brothers and sisters to dancing-school. In the first joyful flash of recognition I cried, 'Oswald, that is my umbrella you are carrying!' whereupon Maria said still more superciliously than before, 'Oh, yes, don't you remember?' (as if reproaching me for my forgetfulness) — 'you gave it to me that Saturday I lunched with you, and it rained so heavily. The boys carry it to school. Where there are children, you can't have too many old umbrellas at hand. They lose them so fast.' She spoke," continued my friend impressively, "as if she were harbouring my umbrella from pure kindness, and because she did not like to wound my feelings by sending it back to me. She made a virtue of giving it shelter."

This is the arrogance which places the borrower, as Charles Lamb discovered long ago, among the great ones of the earth, among those whom their brethren serve. Lamb loved to contrast the "instinctive sovereignty," the frank and open bearing of the man who borrows with the "lean and suspicious" aspect of the man who lends. He stood lost in admiration before the great borrowers of the world, — Alcibiades, Falstaff, Steele, and Sheridan ; an incomparable quartette, to which might be added the shining names of William Godwin and Leigh Hunt. All the characteristic qualities of the class were united, indeed, in Leigh Hunt, as in no other single representative. Sheridan was an unrivalled companion, — could talk seven hours without making even Byron yawn. Steele was the most lovable of spendthrifts. Lending to these men was but a form of investment. They paid in a coinage of their own. But Leigh Hunt combined in the happiest manner a readiness to extract favours with a confirmed habit of never acknowledging the smallest obligation for them. He is a perfect example of the condescending borrower, of the man who permits his friends, as a pleasure to themselves, to relieve his necessities, and who knows nothing of gratitude or loyalty.

It would be interesting to calculate the amount of money which Hunt's friends and acquaintances contributed to his support in life. Shelley gave him at one time fourteen hundred pounds, an amount which the poet could ill spare; and, when he had no more to give, wrote in misery of spirit to Byron, begging a loan for his friend, and promising to repay it, as he feels tolerably sure that Hunt never will. Byron, generous at first, wearied after a time of his position in Hunt's commissariat (it was like pulling a man out of a river, he wrote to Moore, only to see him jump in again), and coldly withdrew. His withdrawal occasioned inconvenience, and has been sharply criticised. Hunt, says Sir Leslie Stephen, loved a cheerful giver, and Byron's obvious reluctance struck him as being in bad taste. His biographers, one and all, have sympathized with this point of view. Even Mr.

Frederick Locker, from whom one would have expected a different verdict, has recorded his conviction that Hunt had probably been "sorely tried" by Byron.

It is characteristic of the preordained borrower, of the man who simply fulfils his destiny in life, that not his obligations only, but his anxieties and mortifications are shouldered by other men. Hunt was care-free and light-hearted; but there is a note akin to anguish in Shelley's petition to Byron, and in his shamefaced admission that he is himself too poor to relieve his friend's necessities. The correspondence of William Godwin's eminent contemporaries teem with projects to alleviate Godwin's needs. His debts were everybody's affair but his own. Sir James Mackintosh wrote to Rogers in the autumn of 1815, suggesting that Byron might be the proper person to pay them. Rogers, enchanted with the idea, wrote to Byron, proposing that the purchase money of "The Siege of Corinth" be devoted to this good purpose. Byron, with less enthusiasm, but resigned, wrote to Murray, directing him to forward the six hundred pounds to Godwin; and Murray, having always the courage of his convictions, wrote back, flatly refusing to do anything of the kind. In the end, Byron used the money to pay his own debts, thereby disgusting everybody but his creditors.

Six years later, however, we find him contributing to a fund which tireless philanthropists were raising for Godwin's relief. On this occasion all men of letters, poor as well as rich, were pressed into active service. Even Lamb, who had nothing of his own, wrote to the painter, Haydon, who had not a penny in the world, and begged him to beg Mrs. Coutts to pay Godwin's rent. He also confessed that he had sent "a very respectful letter" — on behalf of the rent — to Sir Walter Scott; and he explained naïvely that Godwin did not concern himself personally in the matter, because he "left all to his Committee," —a peaceful thing to do.

But how did Godwin come to have a "committee" to raise money for him, when other poor devils had to raise it for themselves, or do without? He was not well-beloved. On the contrary, he bored all whom he did not affront. He was not grateful. On the contrary, he held gratitude to be a vice, as tending to make men "grossly partial" to those who have befriended them. His condescension kept pace with his demands. After his daughter's flight with Shelley, he expressed his just resentment by refusing to accept Shelley's cheque for a thousand pounds unless it were made payable to a third party, unless he could have the money without the formality of an acceptance. Like the great lords of Picardy, who had the "right of credit" from their loyal subjects, Godwin claimed his dues from every chance acquaintance. Crabb Robinson introduced him one evening to a gentleman named Rough. The next day both Godwin and Rough called upon their host, each man expressing his regard for the other, and each asking Robinson if he thought the other would be a likely person to lend him fifty pounds.

There are critics who hold that Haydon excelled all other borrowers known to fame; but his is not a career upon which an admirer of the art can look with pleasure. Haydon's debts hunted him like hounds, and if he pursued borrowing as a means of livelihood,—more lucrative than painting pictures which nobody would buy,—it was only because no third avocation presented itself as a possibility. He is not to be compared for a moment with a true expert like Sheridan, who borrowed for borrowing's sake, and without any sordid motive connected with rents or butchers' bills. Haydon would, indeed, part with his money as readily as if it belonged to him. He would hear an "inward voice" in church, urging him to give his last sovereign; and, having obeyed this voice "with as pure a feeling as ever animated a human heart," he had no resource but immediately to borrow another. It would have been well for him if he could have followed on such occasions the memorable example of Lady Cook, who was so impressed by a begging sermon that she borrowed a sovereign from Sydney Smith to put into the offertory; and — the gold once between her fingers — found herself equally unable to give it or to return it, so went home, a pound richer for her charitable impulse.

Haydon, too, would rob Peter to pay Paul, and rob Paul without paying Peter; but it was all after an intricate and troubled fashion of his own. On one occasion he borrowed ten pounds from Webb. Seven pounds he used to satisfy another creditor, from whom, on the strength of this payment, he borrowed ten pounds more to meet an impending bill. It sounds like a particularly confusing game; but it was a game played in dead earnest, and without the humorous touch which makes the charm of Lady Cook's, or of Sheridan's methods. Haydon would have been deeply grateful to his benefactors, had he not always stood in need of favours to come. Sheridan might perchance have been grateful, could he have remembered who his benefactors were. He laid the world under tribute; and because he had an aversion to opening his mail, — an aversion with which it is impossible not to sympathize, — he frequently made no use of the tribute when it was paid. Moore tells us that James Wesley once saw among a pile of papers on Sheridan's desk an unopened letter of his own, containing a ten-pound note, which he had lent Sheridan some weeks before. Wesley quietly took possession of the letter and the money, thereby raising a delicate, and as yet unsettled, question of morality. Had he a right to those ten pounds because they had once been his, or were they not rather Sheridan's property, destined in the natural and proper order of things never to be returned.

Yet men, even men of letters, have been known to pay their debts, and to restore borrowed property. Moore paid Lord Lansdowne every penny of the generous sum advanced by that nobleman after the defalcation of Moore's deputy in Bermuda. Dr. Johnson paid back ten pounds after a lapse of twenty years, — a pleasant shock to the lender, — and on his death-bed (having fewer sins than most of us to recall) begged Sir Joshua Reynolds to forgive him a trifling loan. It was the too honest return of a pair of borrowed sheets (unwashed) which first chilled Pope's friendship for Lady Mary Wortley Montagu. That excellent gossip, Miss Letitia Matilda Hawkins, who stands responsible for this anecdote, lamented all her life that her father, Sir John Hawkins, could never remember which of the friends borrowed and which lent the offending sheets; but it is a point easily settled in our minds. Pope was probably the last man in Christendom to have been guilty of such a misdemeanour, and Lady Mary was certainly the last woman in Christendom to have been affronted by it. Like Dr. Johnson, she had "no passion for clean linen."

Coleridge, though he went through life leaning his inert weight on other men's shoulders, did remember in some mysterious fashion to return the books he borrowed, enriched often, as Lamb proudly records, with marginal notes which tripled their value. His conduct in this regard was all the more praiseworthy inasmuch as the cobweb statutes which define books as personal property have never met with literal acceptance. Lamb's theory that books belong with the highest propriety to those who understand them best (a theory often advanced in defence of depredations which Lamb would have scorned to commit), was popular before the lamentable invention of printing. The library of Lucullus was, we are told, "open to all," and it would be interesting to know how many precious manuscripts remained ultimately in the great patrician's villa.

Richard Heber, that most princely of collectors, so well understood the perils of his position that he met them bravely by buying three copies of every book,— one for show, one for use, and one for the service of his friends. The position of the show-book seems rather melancholy, but perhaps, in time, it replaced the borrowed volume. Heber's generosity has been nobly praised by Scott, who contrasts the hard-heartedness of other bibliophiles, those "gripple niggards" who preferred holding on to their treasures, with his friend's careless liberality.

Condescension of Borrowers

"Thy volumes, open as thy heart,
Delight, amusement, science, art,
To every ear and eye impart.
Yet who, of all who thus employ them,
Can, like the owner's self, enjoy them?"

The "gripple niggards" might have pleaded feebly in their own behalf that they could not all afford to spend, like Heber, a hundred thousand pounds in the purchase of books; and that an occasional reluctance to part with some hard-earned, hard-won volume might be pardonable in one who could not hope to replace it. Lamb's books were the shabbiest in Christendom; yet how keen was his pang when Charles Kemble carried off the letters of "that princely woman, the thrice noble Margaret Newcastle," an "illustrious folio" which he well knew Kemble would never read. How bitterly he bewailed his rashness in extolling the beauties of Sir Thomas Browne's "Urn Burial" to a guest who was so moved by this eloquence that he promptly borrowed the volume. "But so," sighed Lamb, "have I known a foolish lover to praise his mistress in the presence of a rival more qualified to carry her off than himself."

Johnson cherished a dim conviction that because he read, and Garrick did not, the proper place for Garrick's books was on his — Johnson's — bookshelves; a point which could never be settled between the two friends, and which came near to wrecking their friendship. Garrick loved books with the chilly yet imperative love of the collector. Johnson loved them as he loved his soul. Garrick took pride in their sumptuousness, in their immaculate, virginal splendour. Johnson gathered them to his heart with scant regard for outward magnificence, for the glories of calf and vellum. Garrick bought books. Johnson borrowed them. Each considered that he had a prior right to the objects of his legitimate affection. We, looking back with softened hearts, are fain to think that we should have held our volumes doubly dear if they had lain for a time by Johnson's humble hearth, if he had pored over them at three o'clock in the morning, and had left sundry tokens — grease-spots and spatterings of snuff — upon many a spotless page. But it is hardly fair to censure Garrick for not dilating with these emotions.

Johnson's habit of flinging the volumes which displeased him into remote and dusty corners of the room was ill calculated to inspire confidence, and his powers of procrastination were never more marked than in the matter of restoring borrowed books. We know from Cradock's "Memoirs" how that gentleman, having induced Lord Harborough to lend him a superb volume of manuscripts, containing the poems of James the First, proceeded to re-lend this priceless treasure to Johnson. When it was not returned — as of course it was not — he wrote an urgent letter, and heard to his dismay that Johnson was not only unable to find the book, but that he could not remember having ever received it. The despairing Cradock applied to all his friends for help; and George Steevens, who had a useful habit of looking about him, suggested that a sealed packet, which he had several times observed lying under Johnson's ponderous inkstand, might possibly contain the lost manuscript. Even with this ray of hope for guidance, it never seemed to occur to any one to storm Johnson's fortress, and rescue the imprisoned volume; but after the Doctor's death, two years later, Cradock made a formal application to the executors; and Lord Harborough's property was discovered under the inkstand, unopened, unread, and consequently, as by a happy miracle, uninjured.

Such an incident must needs win pardon for Garrick's churlishness in defending his possessions. "The history of book-collecting," says a caustic critic, "is a history relieved but rarely by acts of pure and undiluted unselfishness." This is true, but are there not virtues so heroic that plain human nature can ill aspire to compass them?

There is something piteous in the futile efforts of reluctant lenders to save their property from depredation. They place their reliance upon artless devices which never yet were known to stay the marauder's hand. They have their names and addresses engraved on foolish little plates, which, riveted to their umbrellas, will, they think, suffice to insure the safety of these useful articles. As well might the border farmer have engraved his name and address on the collars of his grazing herds, in the hope that the riever would respect this symbol of authority. The history of book-plates is largely the history of borrower versus lender. The orderly mind is wont to believe that a distinctive mark, irrevocably attached to every volume, will insure permanent possession. Mr. Gosse, for example, has expressed a touching faith in the efficacy of the book-plate. He has but to explain that he "makes it a rule" never to lend a volume thus decorated, and the would-be borrower bows to this rule as to a decree of fate. "To have a book-plate," he joyfully observes, "gives a collector great serenity and confidence."

Is it possible that the world has grown virtuous without our observing it? Can it be that the old stalwart race of book-borrowers, those "spoilers of the symmetry of shelves," are foiled by so childish an expedient? Imagine Dr. Johnson daunted by a scrap of pasted paper! Or Coleridge, who seldom went through the formality of asking leave, but borrowed armfuls of books in the absence of their legitimate owners! How are we to account for the presence of book-plates — quite a pretty collection at times — on the shelves of men who possess no such toys of their own? When I was a girl I had access to a small and well-chosen library (not greatly exceeding Montaigne's fourscore volumes), each book enriched with an appropriate device of scaly dragon guarding the apples of Hesperides. Beneath the dragon was the motto (Johnsonian in form if not in substance), "Honour and Obligation demand the prompt return of borrowed Books." These words ate into my innocent soul, and lent a pang to the sweetness of possession. Doubts as to the exact nature of "prompt return" made me painfully uncertain as to whether a month, a week, or a day were the limit which Honour and Obligation had set for me. But other and older borrowers were less sensitive, and I have reason to believe that—books being a rarity in that little Southern town—most of the volumes were eventually absorbed by the gaping shelves of neighbours. Perhaps even now (their generous owner long since dead) these worn copies of Boswell, of Elia, of Herrick, and Moore, may still stand forgotten in dark and dusty corners, like gems that magpies hide.

It is vain to struggle with fate, with the elements, and with the borrower; it is folly to claim immunity from a fundamental law, to boast of our brief exemption from the common lot. "Lend therefore cheerfully, O man ordained to lend. When thou seest the proper authority coming, meet it smilingly, as it were halfway." Resistance to an appointed force is but a futile waste of strength.

The Grocer's Cat

Of all animals, the cat alone attains to the Contemplative Life. — ANDREW LANG.

THE grocer's window is not one of those gay and glittering enclosures which display only the luxuries of the table, and which give us the impression that there are favoured classes subsisting exclusively upon Malaga raisins, Russian chocolates, and Nuremberg gingerbread. It is an unassuming window, filled with canned goods and breakfast foods, wrinkled prunes devoid of succulence, and boxes of starch and candles. Its only ornament is the cat, and his beauty is more apparent to the artist than to the fancier. His splendid stripes, black and grey and tawny, are too wide for noble lineage. He has a broad benignant brow, like Benjamin Franklin's; but his brooding eyes, golden, unfathomable, deny benignancy. He is large and sleek, — the grocery mice must be many, and of an appetizing fatness, — and I presume he devotes his nights to the pleasures of the chase. His days are spent in contemplation, in a serene and wonderful stillness, which isolates him from the bustling vulgarities of the street.

Past the window streams the fretful crowd ; in and out of the shop step loud-voiced customers. The cat is as remote as if he were drowsing by the waters of the Nile. Pedestrians pause to admire him, and many of them endeavour, with well-meant but futile familiarity, to win some notice in return. They tap on the window pane, and say, "Halloo, Pussy!" He does not turn his head, nor lift his lustrous eyes. They tap harder, and with more ostentatious friendliness. The stone cat of Thebes could not pay less attention. It is difficult for human beings to believe that their regard can be otherwise than flattering to an animal; but I did see one man intelligent enough to receive this impression. He was a decent and a good-tempered young person, and he had beaten a prolonged tattoo on the glass with the handle of his umbrella, murmuring at the same time vague words of cajolery. Then, as the cat remained motionless, absorbed in revery, and seemingly unconscious of his unwarranted attentions, he turned to me, a new light dawning in his eyes. "Thinks itself some," he said, and I nodded acquiescence. As well try to patronize the Sphinx as to patronize a grocer's cat.

Now, surely this attitude on the part of a small and helpless beast, dependent upon our bounty for food and shelter, and upon our sense of equity for the right to live, is worthy of note, and, to the generous mind, is worthy of respect. Yet there are people who most ungenerously resent it. They say the cat is treacherous and ungrateful, by which they mean that she does not relish unsolicited fondling, and that, like Mr. Chesterton, she will not recognize imaginary obligations. If we keep a cat because there are mice in our kitchen or rats in our cellar, what claim have we to gratitude? If we keep a cat for the sake of her beauty, and because our hearth is but a poor affair without her, she repays her debt with interest when she dozes by our fire. She is the most decorative creature the domestic world can show. She harmonizes with the kitchen's homely comfort, and with the austere seclusion of the library. She gratifies our sense of fitness and our sense of distinction, if we chance to possess these qualities. Did not Isabella d' Este, Marchioness of Mantua, and the finest exponent of distinction in her lordly age, send far and wide for cats to grace her palace? Did she not instruct her agents to make especial search through the Venetian convents, where might be found the deep-furred pussies of Syria and Thibet? Alas for the poor nuns, whose cherished pets were snatched away to gratify the caprice of a great and grasping lady, who habitually coveted all that was beautiful in the world.

The cat seldom invites affection, and still more seldom responds to it. A well-bred tolerance is her nearest approach to demonstration. The dog strives with pathetic insistence to break down the barriers between his intelligence and his master's, to understand and to be understood. The wise cat cherishes her isolation, and permits us to play but a secondary part in her solitary and meditative life. Her intelligence, less facile than the dog's, and far less highly differentiated, owes little to our tutelage; her character has not been moulded by our hands. The changing centuries have left no mark upon her; and, from a past inconceivably remote, she has come down to us, a creature self-absorbed and self-communing, undisturbed by our feverish activity, a dreamer of dreams, a lover of the mysteries of night.

And yet a friend. No one who knows anything about the cat will deny her capacity for friendship. Rationally, without enthusiasm, without illusions, she offers us companionship on terms of equality. She will not come when she is summoned, — unless the summons be for dinner, — but she will come of her own sweet will, and bear us company for hours, sleeping contentedly in her armchair, or watching with half-shut eyes the quiet progress of our work. A lover of routine, she expects to find us in the same place at the same hour every day; and when her expectations are fulfilled (cats have some secret method of their own for telling time), she purrs approval of our punctuality. What she detests are noise, confusion, people who bustle in and out of rooms, and the unpardonable intrusions of the housemaid. On those unhappy days when I am driven from my desk by the iron determination of this maid to "clean up," my cat is as comfortless as I am. Companions in exile, we wander aimlessly to and fro, lamenting our lost hours. I cannot explain to Lux that the fault is none of mine, and I am sure that she holds me to blame.

There is something indescribably sweet in the quiet, self-respecting friendliness of my cat, in her marked predilection for my society. The absence of exuberance on her part, and the restraint I put upon myself, lend an element of dignity to our intercourse. Assured that I will not presume too far on her good nature, that I will not indulge in any of those gross familiarities, those boisterous gambols which delight the heart of a dog, Lux yields herself more and more passively to my persuasions. She will permit an occasional caress, and acknowledge it with a perfunctory purr. She will manifest a patronizing interest in my work, stepping sedately among my papers, and now and then putting her paw with infinite deliberation on the page I am writing, as though the smear thus contributed spelt, "Lux, her mark," and was a reward of merit. But she never curls herself upon my desk, never usurps the place sacred to the memory of a far dearer cat. Some invisible influence restrains her. When her tour of inspection is ended, she returns to her chair by my side, stretching herself luxuriously on her cushions, and watching with steady, sombre stare the inhibited spot, and the little grey phantom which haunts my lonely hours by right of my inalienable love.

Lux is a lazy cat, wedded to a contemplative life. She cares little for play, and nothing for work, — the appointed work of cats. The notion that she has a duty to perform, that she owes service to the home which shelters her, that only those who toil are worthy of their keep, has never entered her head. She is content to drink the cream of idleness, and she does this in a spirit of condescension, wonderful to behold. The dignified distaste with which she surveys a dinner not wholly to her liking, carries confusion to the hearts of her servitors. It is as though Lucullus, having ordered Neapolitan peacock, finds himself put off with nightingales' tongues.

For my own part, I like to think that my beautiful and urbane companion is not a midnight assassin. Her profound and soulless indifference to mice pleases me better than it pleases my household. From an economic point of view, Lux is not worth her salt. Huxley's cat, be it remembered, was never known to attack anything larger and fiercer than a butterfly. "I doubt whether he has the heart to kill a mouse," wrote the proud possessor of this prodigy; "but I saw him catch and eat the first butterfly of the season, and I trust that the germ of courage thus manifested may develop with years into efficient mousing."

Even Huxley was disposed to take a utilitarian view of cathood. Even Cowper, who owed to the frolics of his kitten a few hours' respite from melancholy, had no conception that his adult cat could do better service than slay rats. "I have a kitten, my dear," he wrote to Lady Hesketh, "the drollest of all creatures that ever wore a cat's skin. Her gambols are incredible, and not to be described. She tumbles head over heels several times together. She lays her cheek to the ground, and humps her back at you with an air of most supreme disdain. From this posture she rises to dance on her hind feet, an exercise which she performs with all the grace imaginable; and she closes these various exhibitions with a loud smack of her lips, which, for want of greater propriety of expression, we call spitting. But, though all cats spit, no cat ever produced such a sound as she does. In point of size, she is likely to be a kitten always, being extremely small for her age; but time, that spoils all things, will, I suppose, make her also a cat. You will see her, I hope, before that melancholy period shall arrive; for no wisdom that she may gain by experience and reflection hereafter will compensate for the loss of her present hilarity. She is dressed in a tortoise-shell suit, and I know that you will delight in her."

Had Cowper been permitted to live more with kittens, and less with evangelical clergymen, his hours of gayety might have outnumbered his hours of gloom. Cats have been known to retain in extreme old age the "hilarity" which the sad poet prized. Nature has thoughtfully provided them with one permanent plaything; and Mr. Frederick Locker vouches for a light-hearted old Tom who, at the close of a long and ill-spent life, actually squandered his last breath in the pursuit of his own elusive tail. But there are few of us who would care to see the monumental calm of our fireside sphinx degenerate into senile sportiveness. Better far the measured slowness of her pace, the superb immobility of her repose. To watch an ordinary cat move imperceptibly and with a rhythmic waving of her tail through a doorway (while we are patiently holding open the door), is like looking at a procession. With just such deliberate dignity, in just such solemn state, the priests of Ra filed between the endless rows of pillars into the sunlit temple court.

The cat is a freebooter. She draws no nice distinctions between a mouse in the wainscot, and a canary swinging in its gilded cage. Her traducers, indeed, have been wont to intimate that her preference is for the forbidden quarry ; but this is one of many libellous accusations. The cat, though she has little sympathy with our vapid sentiment, can be taught that a canary is a privileged nuisance, immune from molestation. The bird's shrill notes jar her sensitive nerves. She abhors noise, and a canary's pipe is the most piercing and persistent of noises, welcome to that large majority of mankind which prefers sound of any kind to silence. Moreover, a cage presents just the degree of hindrance to tempt a cat's agility. That Puss habitually refrains from ridding the household of canaries is proof of her innate reasonableness, of her readiness to submit her finer judgment and more delicate instincts to the common caprices of humanity.

As for wild birds, the robins and wrens and thrushes which are predestined prey, there is only one way to save them, the way which Archibald Douglas took to save the honour of Scotland, — "bell the cat." A good-sized sleigh-bell, if she be strong enough to bear it, a bunch of little bells, if she be small and slight, — and the pleasures of the chase are over. One little bell is of no avail, for she learns to move with such infinite precaution that it does not ring until she springs, and then it rings too late. There is an element of cruelty in depriving the cat of sport, but from the bird's point of view the scheme works to perfection. Of course rats and mice are as safe as birds from the claws of a belled cat, but, if we are really humane, we will not regret their immunity.

The boasted benevolence of man is, however, a purely superficial emotion. What am I to think of a friend who anathematizes the family cat for devouring a nest of young robins, and then tells me exultingly that the same cat has killed twelve moles in a fortnight. To a pitiful heart, the life of a little mole is as sacred as the life of a little robin. To an artistic eye, the mole in his velvet coat is handsomer than the robin, which is at best a bouncing, bourgeois sort of bird, a true suburbanite, with all the defects of his class. But my friend has no mercy on the mole because he destroys her garden, — her garden which she despoils every morning, gathering its fairest blossoms to droop and wither in her crowded rooms. To wax compassionate over a bird, and remain hard as flint to a beast, is possible only to humanity. The cat, following her predatory instincts, is at once more logical and less ruthless, because the question of property does not distort her vision. She has none of the vices of civilization.

> "Cats I scorn, who, sleek and fat,
> Shiver at a Norway rat.
> Rough and hardy, bold and free,
> Be the cat that 's made for me;
> He whose nervous paw can take
> My lady's lapdog by the neck,
> With furious hiss attack the hen,
> And snatch a chicken from the pen."

So sang Dr. Erasmus Darwin's intrepid pussy (a better poet than her master) to the cat of Miss Anna Seward, surely the last lady in all England to have encouraged such lawlessness on the part of a — presumably — domestic animal.

For the cat's domesticity is at best only a presumption. It is one of life's ironical adjustments that the creature who fits so harmoniously into the family group should be alien to its influences, and independent of its cramping conditions. She seems made for the fireside she adorns, and where she has played her part for centuries. Lamb, delightedly recording his "observations on cats," sees only their homely qualities. "Put 'em on a rug before the fire, they wink their eyes up, and listen to the kettle, and then purr, which is *their* music." The hymns which Shelley loved were sung by the roaring wind, the hissing kettle, and the kittens purring by his hearth. Heine's cat, curled close to the glowing embers, purred a soft accompaniment to the rhythms pulsing in his brain; but he at least, being a German, was not deceived by this specious show of impeccability. He knew that when the night called, his cat obeyed the summons, abandoning the warm fire for the hard-frozen snow, and the innocent companionship of a poet for the dancing of witches on the hill-tops.

The same grace of understanding — more common in the sixteenth than in the nineteenth century — made the famous Milanese physician, Jerome Cardan, abandon his students at the University of Pavia, in obedience to the decision of his cat. "In the year 1552," he writes with becoming gravity, "having left in the house a little cat of placid and domestic habits, she jumped upon my table, and tore at my public lectures; yet my Book of Fate she touched not, though it was the more exposed to her attacks. I gave up my chair, nor returned to it for eight years." Oh, wise physician, to discern so clearly that "placid and domestic habits" were but a cloak for mysteries too deep to fathom, for warnings too pregnant to be disregarded.

The vanity of man revolts from the serene indifference of the cat. He is forever lauding the dog, not only for its fidelity, which is a beautiful thing, but for its attitude of humility and abasement. A distinguished American prelate has written some verses on his dog, in which he assumes that, to the animal's eyes, he is as God, — a being whose word is law, and from whose sovereign hand flow all life's countless benefactions. Another complacent enthusiast describes *his* dog as sitting motionless in his presence, "at once tranquil and attentive, as a saint should be in the presence of God. He is happy with the happiness which we perhaps shall never know, since it springs from the smile and the approval of a life incomparably higher than his own."

Of course, if we are going to wallow in idolatry like this, we do well to choose the dog, and not the cat, to play the worshipper's part. I am not without a suspicion that the dog is far from feeling the rapture and the reverence which we so delightedly ascribe to him. What is there about any one of us to awaken such sentiments in the breast of an intelligent animal? We have taught him our vices, and he fools us to the top of our bent. The cat, however, is equally free from illusions and from hypocrisy. If we aspire to a petty omnipotence, she, for one, will pay no homage at our shrine. Therefore has her latest and greatest defamer, Maeterlinck, branded her as ungrateful and perfidious. The cat of "The Blue Bird" fawns and flatters, which is something no real cat was ever known to do. When and where did M. Maeterlinck encounter an obsequious cat? That the wise little beast should resent Tyltyl's intrusion into the ancient realms of night, is conceivable, and that, unlike the dog, she should see nothing godlike in a masterful human boy, is hardly a matter for regret; but the most subtle of dramatists should better understand the most subtle of animals, and forbear to rank her as man's enemy because she will not be man's dupe. Rather let us turn back and learn our lesson from Montaigne, serenely playing with his cat as friend to friend, for thus, and thus only, shall we enjoy the sweets of her companionship. If we want an animal to prance on its hind legs, and, with the over-faithful Tylo, cry out, "little god, little god," at every blundering step we take; if we are so constituted that we feel the need of being worshipped by something or somebody, we must feed our vanity as best we can with the society of dogs and men. The grocer's cat, enthroned on the grocer's starch-box, is no fitting friend for us.

As a matter of fact, all cats and kittens, whether royal Persians or of the lowliest estate, resent patronage, jocoseness (which they rightly hold to be in bad taste), and demonstrative affection, —those lavish embraces which lack delicacy and reserve. This last prejudice they carry sometimes to the verge of unkindness, eluding the caresses of their friends, and wounding the spirits of those who love them best. The little eight-year-old English girl who composed the following lines, when smarting from unrequited affection, had learned pretty much all there is to know concerning the capricious nature of cats: —

> "Oh, Selima shuns my kisses!
> Oh, Selima hates her missus!
> I never did meet
> With a cat so sweet,
> Or a cat so cruel as this is."

In such an instance I am disposed to think that Selima's coldness was ill-judged. No discriminating pussy would have shunned the kisses of such an enlightened little girl. But I confess to the pleasure with which I have watched other Selimas extricate themselves from well-meant but vulgar familiarities. I once saw a small black-and-white kitten playing with a judge, who, not unnaturally, conceived that he was playing with the kitten. For a while all went well. The kitten pranced and paddled, fixing her gleaming eyes upon the great man's smirking countenance, and pursued his knotted handkerchief so swiftly that she tumbled head over heels, giddy with her own rapid evolutions. Then the judge, being but human, and ignorant of the wide gap which lies between a cat's standard of good taste and the lenient standard of the court-room, ventured upon one of those doubtful pleasantries which a few pussies permit to privileged friends, but which none of the race ever endure from strangers. He lifted the kitten by the tail until only her forepaws touched the rug, which she clutched desperately, uttering a loud protesting mew. She looked so droll in her helplessness and wrath that several members of the household (her own household, which should have known better) laughed outright, — a shameful thing to do.

Here was a social crisis. A little cat of

manifestly humble origin, with only an innate sense of propriety to oppose to a coarse-minded magistrate, and a circle of mocking friends. The judge, imperturbably obtuse, dropped the kitten on the rug, and prepared to resume their former friendly relations. The kitten did not run away, she did not even walk away; that would have been an admission of defeat. She sat down very slowly, as if first searching for a particular spot in the intricate pattern of the rug, turned her back upon her former playmate, faced her false friends, and tucked her outraged tail carefully out of sight. Her aspect was that of a cat alone in a desert land, brooding over the mystery of her nine lives. In vain the handkerchief was trailed seductively past her little nose, in vain her contrite family spoke words of sweetness and repentance. She appeared as aloof from her surroundings as if she had been wafted to Arabia; and presently began to wash her face conscientiously and methodically, with the air of one who finds solitude better than the companionship of fools. Only when the judge had put his silly handkerchief into his pocket, and had strolled into the library under the pretence of hunting for a book which he had never left there, did the kitten close her eyes, lower her obdurate little head, and purr herself tranquilly to sleep.

A few years afterwards I was permitted to witness another silent combat, another signal victory. This time the cat was, I grieve to say, a member of a troupe of performing animals, exhibited at the Folies-Bergère in Paris. Her fellow actors, poodles and monkeys, played their parts with relish and a sense of fun. The cat, a thing apart, condescended to leap twice through a hoop, and to balance herself very prettily on a large rubber ball. She then retired to the top of a ladder, made a deft and modest toilet, and composed herself for slumber.

Twice the trainer spoke to her persuasively, but she paid no heed, and evinced no further interest in him nor in his entertainment. Her time for condescension was past.

The next day I commented on the cat's behaviour to some friends who had also been to the Folies-Bergère on different nights. "But," said the first friend, "the evening I went, that cat did wonderful things; came down the ladder on her ball, played the fiddle, and stood on her head."

"Really," said the second friend. "Well, the night *I* went, she did nothing at all except cuff one of the monkeys that annoyed her. She just sat on the ladder, and watched the performance. I presumed she was there by way of decoration."

All honour to the cat, who, when her little body is enslaved, can still preserve the freedom of her soul. The dogs and the monkeys obeyed their master; but the cat, like Montaigne's happier pussy long ago, had "her time to begin or to refuse," and showman and audience waited upon her will.

THE END

The Riverside Press
CAMBRIDGE . MASSACHUSETTS
U . S . A